W

THINK
BOOKS

THINK
BOOKS

A Think Book
First published in Great Britain in 2005 by
Think Books
The Pall Mall Deposit
124-128 Barlby Road, London W10 6BL
www.think-books.com

Text © Think Publishing 2005
Design and layout © Think Publishing 2005
The moral rights of the author have been asserted

Editor: Sonja Patel
Writers: Rhiannon Guy and Matt Packer
Designer: Lou Millward
The Why? team: James Collins, Emma Jones, John Innes,
Mark Searle, Dominic Scott, Jes Stanfield, Sarah Watson

All rights reserved. No part of this publication may be reproduced, stored in a retrieval system, or transmitted in any form or by any means, electronic, mechanical, photocopying, recording or otherwise, without the prior permission of the copyright holder.
A CIP catalogue record for this book is available from the British Library.
ISBN 1-84525-009-5

Printed & bound in Great Britain by William Clowes Ltd, Beccles, Suffolk.
The publishers and authors have made every effort to ensure the accuracy and currency of the information in Why?. The publisher and authors disclaim any liability, loss, injury or damage incurred as a consequence, directly or indirectly, of the use and application of the contents of this book.

Why?

'The important thing is not to stop questioning.
Curiosity has its own reason for existing.'
ALBERT EINSTEIN

Why? thanks to...

Freire Barnes, Gemma Clunie, Lauren Edwards, Rawia Edwards, Dinny Gollop, Katie Goodall, Lucy Hellberg, Marie Jobelius, Mac Nicoll, Keren Packer, Nigel Packer, Pat Packer, Helen Smale, Miria Swain and Toby Wagstaff.

THEY ALL KNOW WHY

Why? are we here...

If you've ever been lost for words at a dinner party, longed to dazzle in a debate or wanted to show off your devastating database of general knowledge on a date, then *Why?* is for you. This socially sparkling conversation companion provides you with the elusive answers – or at least a witty one-liner – to over 100 of the world's most puzzling questions; the ones that should evoke a straightforward response but always seem to get away. Compact enough to transport to any occasion, and divided into eight easy-to-navigate chapters to aid an annoyingly speedy response (while you slip around the corner to quickly look it up of course), this pocket-sized 'enwhyclopedia' is the essential undercover tool for impressing your friends – and showing up the competition along the way. A quizzical compendium of need-to-know facts and tantalisingly superfluous trivia – with sections on natural happenings, human beings, everyday inventions, food, wildlife, words, traditions and puzzling pastimes – if you really want to know *Why?* don't leave home without it!

Sonja Patel, Editor

Why? contents

NATURE'S WAY	Page 11
IT'S ONLY HUMAN	Page 25
WILDLIFE WONDERS	Page 53
CRYPTIC CATCHPHRASES	Page 67
PUZZLING PASTIMES	Page 93
FOOD FOR THOUGHT	Page 107
TALL TRADITIONS	Page 125
MAN-MADE MYSTERIES	Page 143

Nature's way

FROM WHY IS THE SKY BLUE?
TO WHY IS THE DEAD SEA SALTY?

Why is the sky blue?

THE KNOWING REPLY
Oxygen atoms in the air scatter blue light over us like a huge canopy.

THE DEEP AND MEANINGFUL
Hold a prism in front of a beam of sunlight (or if it's dark, a copy of Pink Floyd's *Dark Side of the Moon* will do, although the drawing is, in fact, technically wrong). From the rainbow that appears, you'll see that blue is one of the colours or light wavelengths of the spectrum that we can see with our eyes. Oxygen atoms in the air are of a similar size to a wavelength of blue light, so they can interact with it and scatter it over us like a canopy; while longer wavelength colours like red pass straight through the air into the upper atmosphere. This blue canopy is the sky and our eyes pick it up from millions of different angles. Which prompts the further questions: Can I bottle it? Why does it sometimes look pink? and Could Jimi Hendrix really kiss the sky?

Why is the Earth round?

THE KNOWING REPLY

Gravity makes it round, although the Earth's rotation pulls it slightly out of shape. So technically it's not. Which still doesn't mean it's square or flat!

THE DEEP AND MEANINGFUL

The Earth is round for the same reason that all the planets are round – gravity won't let it be anything else. Think of gravity as a force that points toward the centre of the planet so that every part of the surface is pulled evenly inward, resulting in a spherical shape. The technical name for this is isostatic adjustment. What many people don't know, or remember, is that the Earth isn't a true sphere, for a couple of reasons. Once every 24 hours, the rotation of the earth causes an apparent centrifugal force which creates a bulge at the equator and forces it to squash out of shape; in fact, the earth's diameter at the equator is greater than the diameter between the poles. Mountains and valleys and man-made structures like skyscrapers also get in the way of geometric perfection; plus as planets get larger, gravity gets stronger, until eventually large objects on the surface are crushed under their own weight. That's why there are no 1,000-mile-high mountains or skyscrapers that are 3,000 storeys tall, and of course, why giants don't exist...

Why does ice sometimes appear white and sometimes clear?

THE KNOWING REPLY
Tiny irregularities in the ice scatter light to make it appear white.

THE DEEP AND MEANINGFUL
Clear substances, which appear white, usually have to be broken down into small grains, with more combined surfaces from which to scatter light, like caster sugar or the whiteness of powdery snow. However, solid ice appears white because of large-scale irregularities in it which can also scatter light – in this case, large-scale doesn't mean rocks, mountains, skyscrapers or elephants but anything even minutely bigger than a wavelength of visible light. That's about 1/2000 of a millimetre and includes air bubbles, dust, dirt and stress cracks from strain as the ice is freezing. When the ice looks blue or milky this is caused by even smaller irregularities, which cause a different type of scattering, leaving a strange, surreal glow. White or blue ice is also cleverly designed to help humans see where they are going so they don't trip.

Why is it that when things get wet they get darker, even though water is clear?

THE KNOWING REPLY
Water in fabric absorbs light waves, which makes the wet patch appear darker than the surface around it.

THE DEEP AND MEANINGFUL
To shed some light on this one, you need to excuse the wet bit for the moment, and imagine that whether an object appears dark or not is actually something of an optical illusion. When light waves from the sun or a man-made source hit the surface of an absorbent material when it's wet - that is, full of water molecules - some of them cannot be absorbed and so scatter back or reflect from the water. Some light waves don't make it back to our eyes, while others are refracted or bent in a different direction, which makes the wet patch appear darker than the surface around it. So next time you spill some beer on your trousers, all you have to do is turn out the light!

Why are leaves usually green, and why do they turn red in autumn?

THE KNOWING REPLY
In fact, they are actually multicoloured all year round.

THE DEEP AND MEANINGFUL
Pick up a random handful of different coloured leaves and you'll see that small amounts of pigment are present in them all year round. During spring and summer, leaves appear more green because of the high levels of chlorophyll (the stuff that plants use to capture sunlight for photosynthesis so they can make their own food) present. The amount of chlorophyll is so high during the summer that the green colour blockades all other pigments in the leaf; but as the days grow shorter in the fall, chlorophyll production slows down and eventually stops. This is when the yellow, brown and rusty pigments - provided by carotenoids and anthocyanins - become visible. In some trees, like maples, glucose is trapped in the leaves after photosynthesis stops, which sunlight and the cool nights of autumn turn into a red colour. In others, the brownish hue of autumnal oak leaves, for example, is made from waste left in the leaves. Leaf colour is also a great way to check what time of year it is - and how our climate is changing!

Why does lightning never strike twice in the same place?

THE KNOWING REPLY
Nothing could be more wrong than this old proverb.

THE DEEP AND MEANINGFUL
Although the less literal meaning of this old proverb - first recorded by one PH Myers in 1857 - implies that the same misfortune will not happen twice, lightning actually frequently strikes twice in the same place. Buildings such as the Empire State Building have been hit hundreds of times and can be struck several times in the same storm. Tall buildings, towers and antennae are more likely to be hit by lightning as they are closer to the sky and provide an easy way for the lightning to find something conductive to get to earth quickly - much quicker than just travelling through the air. It is technically unlikely for a low level spot to be hit twice in the same storm, but it is by no means impossible and does happen. If the lightning has used one route to conduct through, it is because it is the easiest and quickest way for it to travel and so the laws of physics mean that the same path may well be followed again. If you're worried about being hit again, keep those gum boots on.

Why do we have different climates at the poles and the equator?

THE KNOWING REPLY
How much energy we absorb from the sun depends on latitude and time of year due to the rotation and axis of the Earth.

THE DEEP AND MEANINGFUL
As most sunseekers know, the nearer you get to the equator, the hotter you get. This is because the sun shines from almost overhead. At the North and South Poles, even when the sun is above the horizon, its light is coming at an angle. This means that the sunlight is spread out over more area and can't warm the ground as much, hence the poles are the coldest places on Earth. This is because the Earth orbits the sun every 365 days, but also rotates on its own axis – spinning at an angle of 23.5° to the vertical – once every 24 hours. The spinning gives us night, day and annual seasons, while the Earth's angle to the sun determines how warm it is at different latitudes across each hemisphere. Interestingly, this 'warmer at the equator' effect takes place on most known planets apart from Venus: here the thick atmosphere traps heat, causing a runaway greenhouse effect and planet-wide scorching temperatures of 450°C, day and night. Is this the blueprint for our future Earth…?

Why does the sun rise in the east and set in the west?

THE KNOWING REPLY

It takes 24 hours for the Earth to complete one full rotation in an easterly direction, meaning the sun appears to roll across the sky from east to west.

THE DEEP AND MEANINGFUL

The Egyptians built all their towns on the east bank of the Nile, and all their tombs on the west because of it; the Greeks and Romans explained it as the sun god Helios heading west on his golden chariot of fire and then catching the boat back ready to start again in the morning; and the English pagans are widely thought to have built Stonehenge in homage to it, if the summer solstice at Glastonbury is anything to go by. In fact, this powerful yet everyday phenomenon doesn't just happen to the sun, but to the moon, the planets and the stars too; and all because the earth spins to the east. Suppose you are facing east - the planet carries you eastward as it turns, so whatever lies beyond that eastern horizon eventually comes up over the horizon and you see it! As the Earth rotates, the sun appears to sweep across the sky from east to west, and the path it follows changes from season to season.

Why is the Dead Sea salty?

THE KNOWING REPLY
Because it has no tributaries or rivers to carry the salt away; evaporation into the sky simply leaves even more salt behind.

THE DEEP AND MEANINGFUL
Originally, the Dead Sea – which has a composition of roughly 31.5% salt – was not an inland sea but one connected to bigger oceans. Around three million years ago the whole area of the Jordan Valley was flooded by water from the Mediterranean. Geological evidence suggests that about two million years ago, the land between the Dead Sea and the Mediterranean rose, thereby forming an inland sea or lake. The sediment that collected on the bottom of the lake which was much heavier than the salt deposits, forced the salt higher and nearer the water, creating the saltiness. When the floor of the sea fell even further, salt domes and cliffs were created. The reason it stays salty is because it has no outlet apart from evaporation which leaves salty deposits. Other seas, like the Mediterranean, have somewhere for the water to escape. The saltier the sea, the easier it is to float... but that's another question.

Why are bubbles round?

THE KNOWING REPLY

Because spheres are the shape that bubbles need to assume to survive.

THE DEEP AND MEANINGFUL

Lift a bubble wand to your mouth and blow gently. As you blow, you are forcing the soap molecules to stretch around the air you are puffing into them. The soap molecules want to hold together and need a small surface area to do so effectively. The geometric form with the least surface area is the sphere, so bubbles will always be round. If you are a competent bubble blower, you can show off by creating a bubble that is not round. Try to blow a cluster of bubbles. Within the soapy mass, the centre bubble will alter shape due to the pressure of its surrounding friends; it may well even form a cube. Pop the surrounding bubbles before the whole thing floats off or bursts, and you will see the remaining centre one revert to a sphere. Magic!

Why don't we see rainbows at midday?

THE KNOWING REPLY

Unless you spend lunchtime pushing the sun to new angles, you're out of luck.

THE DEEP AND MEANINGFUL

Rainbows are very picky about conditions before they show up, and their most pressing demand is that the sun be in the right place. Try to imagine the atmosphere as a kind of natural cinema. If we're going to see a rainbow, we need to be facing into the storm (the screen) with the sun blazing from its crack in the clouds behind us (the projector). Imagine your own shadow thrown out before you as you gaze into the veil of misty rain. The shadow of your head marks the antisolar point: the spot directly opposite the sun. A rainbow forms in an atmospheric region between 40° and 42° from the antisolar point – which means that if the sun is any higher than 42°, it won't be able to project its light at the correct angle for a rainbow to form. At around midday, the sun is at its highest, so that effectively rules out rainbows until the afternoon. Like pixels on a TV screen, raindrops decide a rainbow's resolution. Larger drops will reveal strong red, green and violet hues. Finer rain tones down red. In fog, rainbows can appear as ghostly bands, spooky cousins of the multicolored ones, called fogbow. Brrrr...

Why do weather forecasters get it wrong?

THE KNOWING REPLY

Weather it will or weather it won't changes very quickly over time.

THE DEEP AND MEANINGFUL

I mean, honestly, in the 21st century just how hard is it to stick your head out of the window and work out if it's sunny or rainy? Well, actually it's pretty complex and, given meteorology isn't an exact science, accuracy does suffer. Also, since forecasts are usually national, generalisations are inevitable, and so reports will be less accurate. The weather can change very quickly and information can soon become out of date. This means a television forecast can already be inaccurate by the time it has got to air from the meteorology recordings. In the face of public demand for guidance on whether (excuse the pun) or not to take their brolly to work, forecasters do their best and give as much information as possible. Perhaps it is worth sparing a thought for forecasters from Moscow who faced fines by Mayor Yuri Luzhkov for every prediction they got wrong. Surely it was always cold...

Why does water swirl down the plug hole in different directions depending on which hemisphere you're in?

THE KNOWING REPLY
The only thing spinning in the wrong direction is the question.

THE DEEP AND MEANINGFUL
Enamoured by the idea that even bathrooms could be affected by the great north-south divide, scientists in the 1960s were eager to attribute this amazing phenomenon to a gravitational effect known as the Coriolis Force. French mathematician Gaspard de Coriolis discovered in 1835 that the earth's rotation appears to deflect air in the atmosphere to the left or to the right, depending which side of the equator you are standing on and how near you are to the poles. The amount of deflection the air makes is directly related to the speed at which it is moving and its latitude; hence cyclones spin clockwise in the southern hemisphere, while in the north they spin anti-clockwise. When it comes to the bathtub debate, this theory is washed down the plug hole: as any hemisphere-hopping traveller can tell you, you can over-ride the supposed Coriolis Force by using your finger to force the water down the other way.

It's only human

FROM WHY IS YAWNING CONTAGIOUS?
TO WHY DO OUR STOMACHS RUMBLE?

Why do we have appendixes if they don't actually do anything?

THE KNOWING REPLY
It's a bacterial filter! Vs. It stands between us and the apes!

THE DEEP AND MEANINGFUL
In the past scientists claimed that there were over 180 vestigial – that is, redundant or useless – organs in or on the human body, including the appendix, the tonsils, the tail bone and the thymus. The ensuing debate seems to be largely linked to which side of the how-did-we-get-here? fence you sit on. Some creationists argue that the appendix is simply a trouble-making organ designed solely to cause humans discomfort, thereby implying its technical uselessness; while some evolutionists argue that if total absence of the appendix were a token of advancement, the old and new world monkeys would be considered more highly evolved than mankind. To back up the latter argument, studies have shown that the appendix could be part of the immune system, strategically located between the entrance of the almost sterile ileum and the usually high bacterial content of the colon. Either way, unless yours flares up, it's probably wise to leave it that way.

Why don't you get a tan on the soles of your feet or the palms of your hands?

THE KNOWING REPLY
There's not enough pigment in them to help them change colour,
possibly because we used to walk on all fours.

THE DEEP AND MEANINGFUL
It's all down to the very important matter of pigment and its main task of protection. Most of our skin contains pigment cells caused melanocytes, which produce a substance called melanin. Like a natural SPF, the pigment melanin absorbs the UV radiation in sunlight to help protect our skin from damage. A tan occurs when, in response to harmful UV rays, melanin attempts to protect your skin from burning. While the upsurge in skin cancer is proof that extensive sun exposure debilitates skin, those born with a higher level of melanin, resulting in naturally darker skin, will naturally be better protected from sunburn. The reason the soles of our hands and feet don't tan is because they contain a minimal level of melanocytes and therefore less pigment. Some evolutionists say this is because we once roamed the land as apes and were designed to walk on all fours. Consequently, our hands and feet were seldom exposed to the sun and didn't need pigment protection.

Why do some old men have hair in their ears and noses?

THE KNOWING REPLY
It's a hirsute off-shoot of the hormone somatotrophin, which increases with age.

THE DEEP AND MEANINGFUL
Like a last raucous laugh from whoever drew up the blueprint for human design, this hairy and humiliating syndrome is stimulated by a cheeky little growth hormone called somatotrophin, or SH. For some poor folk, SH secretion increases with age, and, coupled with an overdrive of male sex hormones, or androgens, in the twilight years, causes hair to go wild. The only good news for afflicted gentleman (aside from the technology of nostril and ear clippers) is that it happens to women too, from a downy complexion to the odd whisker and even a full-grown beard. An ageist little number, escalating SH is also the culprit behind bigger lips, bulbous noses, fat fingers and thickening ear lobes. 'All the better to hear you with,' said Grandma...

Why does your mouth 'water' when you're about to eat a meal?

THE KNOWING REPLY
Your senses have told your brain to start producing enzymes which, along with 'water', help break food down into nutrients your body can absorb.

THE DEEP AND MEANINGFUL
During mechanical digestion, the teeth break the food into smaller bits, while your taste buds detect the chemicals that make up the food you are eating and secrete the appropriate enzymes through your digestive system. Your mouth 'waters' just before you eat something because your super-sensitive eyes, nose and mouth send a message to your brain telling it to start producing salivary amylase to help break down starches (from carbs like bread and pasta) in your anticipated food. Saliva also contains salivary lipase which your body secretes continuously and accumulates in the stomach between meals. This hydrolyzes (dissolves in water) any dietary fat in your food and breaks it down into fatty acids and glycerol. After all this, your tongue pushes the chewed food to the back of your throat, and you swallow it down your oesophagus. Salivary amylase stops – and so does your mouth watering.

Why is yawning contagious?

THE KNOWING REPLY
Actually, only 40%-60% of people find yawning contagious. Let's face it, when it comes to communicating a soporific mind there's no better way.

THE DEEP AND MEANINGFUL
Cats and chimpanzees do it, fish and dogs do it, even 11-week old fetuses do it. While for the 40%-60% of people who studies have shown find yawning contagious, seeing one person yawn can be enough to set off a whole room. Such is the power of the yawn that thinking about it, hearing someone yawn and even reading about yawning can trigger a reaction – in fact you're probably yawning your head off right now. However, the ability to agree on a theory doesn't seem to be as contagious as the yawn. The Physiological Theory says that our bodies induce hypoxia, or yawning to draw in more oxygen or remove a build-up of carbon dioxide. The larger the group of people, the more carbon dioxide we need to get rid of, the more people yawn. However, on the premise of non-yawning exercise, this theory has already been yawned out of class. The Evolution Theory stipulates that we used to yawn to bare our teeth; and yawning back is simply fighting back. And then, of course, there's the The Boredom Theory, cited as the main root of yawning along with fatigue and drowsiness. One can only assume that boredom and tiredness are contagious too.

Why do we get goose pimples?

THE KNOWING REPLY
Our fight or flight reflex causes so-called piloerection of the skin, which strangely enough doesn't happen in geese!

THE DEEP AND MEANINGFUL
Goose pimples or goose bumps in humans are caused by our inbuilt reaction to strong emotions, like fear, anger or even excited anticipation. This is usually called fight or flight, which means our instincts tell us to put 'em up or fly away. The flight/goose connection is strictly a coincidence, as the vestigial goose bump is actually a by-product of the days when it was believed that we were made with rather a nice coat of fur. Look at any hairy mammal today and you'll notice how his coat puffs out when he's scared, angry or cold. The erect hairs serve a dual purpose of making him seem larger to ward off predators and trapping air to create a layer of insulation. This is called piloerection and if we still had a coat of fur this would happen to us too; instead our skin stands on end where the hair should be. The geese came into it in medieval times, when someone compared the reaction to a plump bird's bare plucked skin after quills and down were removed five times a year for market. While geese puff out their feathers in the cold, only animals with fur or spines can get piloerection. Just in case you thought you could fly away...

Why can't babies cry inside the womb?

THE KNOWING REPLY
Mother Nature helps babies breathe, but also stops them from making sound.

THE DEEP AND MEANINGFUL
The reason why babies can't cry, or make any sound, within the womb is because the miraculous tools of nature that keep them alive restrict them from doing so. While in the womb, babies' lungs are full of amniotic fluid, which they filter into their respiratory organs as they develop. So, with blocked respiratory systems and no fresh air around until they are born, foetuses are unable to draw breath. And if they can't draw breath, they can't cry. However, that's not to say that they can't go through the motions. Ultrasound technology developed by UK scientists has shown babies yawning, smiling and even crying inside the womb, their facial expressions revealing their moods very clearly. Well, they do say practice makes perfect...

Why can't we hum with a blocked nose?

THE KNOWING REPLY
Contrary to popular belief, we hum through our noses, not our mouths.

THE DEEP AND MEANINGFUL
Hmmmmmmm... does it sound like that humming is coming from your mouth? In fact the sound that we hear is of our vocal vibrations resonating in our closed mouths before the air from our lungs carries the sound through our noses. Our vocal chords can't vibrate unless a steady stream of air is making them - so if we pinch our noses, we block off the sound. One recent Swedish study even suggested that humming could actually fend off respiratory illness reporting that: 'Since humming increases sinus ventilation dramatically, we speculate that daily periods of humming could be helpful to prevent sinusitis where bad ventilation is part of the disease process.' Hmmm indeed!

Why do we get bags under our eyes?

THE KNOWING REPLY
Some dermatologists believe that dead tissue from starved blood cells builds up with age and through bad habits; water retention is another theory.

THE DEEP AND MEANINGFUL
If you've got some unwanted matching luggage under your eyes, no amount of miracle skin creams or magic potions will help; you need to look on what goes on inside. The skin under our eyes is very thin and sensitive, so it loosens earlier in our lives than other areas. While you can't turn back the clock, you can help prevent this loosening by protecting blood vessels from dying out – caused by smoking, bad nutrition or over-exposure to harmful sunlight – and therefore prevent a build up of dead tissue under the eye. Other studies show that when the fat from the area around the eye-socket droops down into the region below, it begins to retain water. This creates an appearance of puffiness, which gives the impression of sunken eyes. The only thing you can do for under-eye luggage is increase your intake of antioxidants (green, leafy veg and vitamin-rich fruit), stay out of the sun, sleep more and stop smoking. Trying to cry the water out will just make it worse.

Why do some people have dimples?

THE KNOWING REPLY
Give the fated ones a break: those cutesy creases are in their genes.

THE DEEP AND MEANINGFUL
Often considered to be the first sign of an ill-fated child star, dimples on the cheeks around the mouth come down the simple matter of dimple genes. Your physical features are represented by two genes, one from mum and one from dad; and paired up as either two dominant genes, a dominant and a recessive gene, or two recessive genes. In order to inherit a distinctive feature, like a Kirk Douglas or a Shirley Temple, a face full of freckles or of course, dimples, you need one dominant gene, namely the one called 'D' – for dimples. In contrast, smooth sorts born without dimples have been saddled with the recessive, 'dd' gene, a shorthand for 'dimples denied'.

Why do some people feel strange during a full moon?

THE KNOWING REPLY
Scientists can find no physical reason for their lunacy.

THE DEEP AND MEANINGFUL
Human beings have been pinning their bad behaviour on the full moon for centuries – the word lunatic stemming from luna, the Latin word for moon. In addition to the 28-day cycle shared by the moon and women of a fertile age, the fact that the human body is 80% water largely contributes to the notion that the moon should have a powerful effect on the human body, and therefore an effect on behaviour. In fact, the moon only affects unbounded bodies of water, such as the 80% of water on the earth's surface, which is why our tides flow to and fro. Our bodies just don't work like this. According to one astronomer, 'a mosquito would exert more gravitational pull on your arm than the moon would'. Despite several studies to back this up, the poor moon has still been linked to crime, suicide, mental illness, natural disasters, accidents, fertility and that old chestnut, the werewolf. Perhaps when we stop trying to find life on the moon, we'll be able to find our own.

Why don't we speak the same language if we're all part of the same species?

THE KNOWING REPLY
It could be punishment for the Tower of Babel, or evolution and migration combined. Just another example of the many languages we speak!

THE DEEP AND MEANINGFUL
There are 6,912 known living languages in the world – five are spoken by 50% of the world's population, another 100 by 45%, and 1,000 are spoken on Papua New Guinea alone. So where did they all come from, and wouldn't it be easier to stick with one? According to Christian creationists, the splintering of so-called Adamic, or Adam's 'father tongue', was God's punishment for humans building the Tower of Babel. Over in the evolutionary corner, it's believed that language began millions of years ago as a way of warning fellow hunters of danger, or as a social lubricant for women who were left working at home – perhaps one reason why girls usually learn to speak earlier than boys. The scientist and linguist camp theorises that constant migration, changing environments and evolving lifestyles created new speech forms. Languages like Esperanto did try to break the mould, but our love of 'listening to our own voice' means even more new languages are being invented as we speak.

Why don't we laugh when we tickle our own ribs?

THE KNOWING REPLY
The essential ingredient for laughing from a tickle is the element of surprise. So give up on yourself and have fun tickling someone else instead.

THE DEEP AND MEANINGFUL
Most of us have a ticklish spot somewhere on our bodies. For some it's just above the knee, for others it's the back of the neck, and some of us go into fits of laughter if someone grabs our sides. Laughing when another person tickles you is a natural reflex reaction, stemming from a primal defence system designed to register unease when ambushed by creepy crawlies like spiders or bugs, and panic for more fatal predators. Back to the present day, if you grab yourself by the sides in an attempt to tickle yourself, the cerebellum part of the brain – the bit that registers our movements – anticipates this contact from the hands and prepares itself for it. No element of surprise, no tickle; but more to the point, what about all those strange folk who don't feel tickles at all… are they, in fact, even human?

Why does looking at the sun cause some people to sneeze?

THE KNOWING REPLY
The many nerve endings in the brain are sometimes linked and bright light can stimulate a sneezing reflex.

THE DEEP AND MEANINGFUL
The sun sneeze, or photic sneeze, is not just restricted to the sun, it can also be triggered by looking at a very bright light bulb. A fairly common and relatively harmless condition, affecting as many as one in four people, photic sneezing also seems to run in families, although a photic sneezing gene has not yet been found. While normal sneezing is a reflex action of the body designed to get rid of something that is irritating the inside of the nose, like dust, pollen or germs, the photic sneeze does not seem to help protect the body in any way. One theory suggests that a sudden bright flash of light could cause the nerve signal from the eye along the optic nerve to trigger the nearby trigeminal nerve – that's the one that controls sneezing. One scientist has even given the condition a name: Autosomal Dominant Compelling Helio-Ophthalmic Outburst, or ACHOO for short.

Why do we have eyebrows?

THE KNOWING REPLY
Like hairy visors for the eyes, eyebrows keep the sweat at bay.

THE DEEP AND MEANINGFUL
Evolutionists think eyebrows were originally designed to keep the sweat and rain out of your eyes. The forehead or brow is a perspiration hotspot, and as sweat is salty the cleverly arched eyebrows are a necessary defence against a salty river stinging your eyes and impeding your vision. Back in the days of early man these functions would have helped us survive, as eyebrows could preserve vision while you were running away from a predator or trying to find shelter in a storm. These days eyebrows are not so key to survival; and with the amount of over-grooming that goes on, it's a good job!

Why do we only use 10% of our brains?

THE KNOWING REPLY

It's a myth! We use all of our brains.

THE DEEP AND MEANINGFUL

A more pertinent question would probably be why do some people continue to believe this myth? As PET (Positron Emission Tomography) and MRI (Magnetic Resonance Imaging) scans have proved that we do, in fact, use all of our brain, it might seem that these people are just not trying hard enough! True, some functions of the human body only use a small part of the brain, but most everyday activities typically involve it all. Some people think the myth may have originated from an Albert Einstein misquotation. Others cite the misinterpretation of the work of French physiologist Pierre Flourens in the 1800s, or a quote by the writer William James who wrote: 'We are making use of only a small part of our possible mental and physical resources.' This, along with some studies in the 1920s, then triggered advertising copy like the 1930s slogan, 'Scientists say you only use one-tenth of your brain. Wake up to your true potential'. Apparently, Uri Geller is such a fan of this statement he uses it as one of the explanations why he can bend spoons! Presumably his full potential lies in the 90% of his brain he doesn't use.

Why do pregnant women gain 30lbs when the average baby weighs 7lbs?

THE KNOWING REPLY
When they say she's eating for two, they really mean it!

THE DEEP AND MEANINGFUL
Even though the average baby weighs about 7lbs, the rest of the weight that the mother carries around during pregnancy can be accounted for as follows: baby, 7lbs; extra blood to help the baby grow, 3lbs; extra breast tissue to produce milk, 2lbs; placenta to link baby to mum while in the womb, 1.5lbs; amniotic fluid to help respirate the baby, 2lbs; increased uterine muscle to help hold the baby and push it out, 2lbs; retained water to help keep the baby comfortable, 4lbs; maternal stores of nutrients, proteins and fats, 7lbs. Mums-to-be who thought they could stuff their face with sweets while pregnant, think again. It doesn't leave much room for pies, doughnuts or chocolate!

Why do our fingers and toes become prune-like in the bath?

THE KNOWING REPLY
Prolonged exposure to water washes usually waterproof sebum off the epidermis, forcing loose parts of the skin to swell.

THE DEEP AND MEANINGFUL
Your skin is made up of two layers. The outer layer is called the epidermis and the lower level is the dermis. The epidermis produces an oily substance called sebum – touch a window or mirror and you'll see your oily fingerprint there. One of sebum's jobs is to keep your skin waterproof, a job it usually does very well. After long periods of time in a swimming pool, shower or bathtub, however, much of this sebum is washed off and your epidermis starts to absorb water and swell. The so-called pruning happens where parts of your epidermis are 'tied down' or anchored to your dermis and subsequently cannot expand. Luckily your skin is able to dry out and re-sebum itself, so you don't walk around with a permanent set of prunes!

Why do we lose our sense of taste when we lose our sense of smell?

THE KNOWING REPLY
Because the receptors in our noses are more numerous and much more finely tuned than the ones in our mouths.

THE DEEP AND MEANINGFUL
The mouth is a pretty basic instrument of taste. It recognises only the flavours: salt, sweet, bitter, sour, and, some scientists claim, glutamate. The nose, on the other hand, is a refined and sensitive connoisseur. It is our olfactory senses that tell us whether food is fruity, spicy, flowery, resinous, foul or burned. When you take a mouthful, odour molecules from the food travel through the passage between your nose and mouth to olfactory receptor cells at the top of your nasal cavity. If you have a blocked nose or happen to be wearing a clothes peg (synchronised swimmers or sewage workers often do), air and odour molecules can't reach your olfactory receptor cells. This means your brain receives no signal identifying the smell, and everything tastes similar. Texture, temperature and basic tastes can be recognised by the mouth, but the nuance of flavour is lost.

Why don't the hairs on our arms get split ends like the ones on our heads?

THE KNOWING REPLY
Arm hair is programmed to stay short, so doesn't grow long enough to split.

THE DEEP AND MEANINGFUL
The short and long of it is that arm hair never flows mane-like enough to develop split ends. But that just leads to another question about why arm hair is so short. At the root of each hair follicle, new hair cells form and push older cells out. As they're pushed out, the cells die and become hair. Each follicle creates new cells for a certain period of time, officially known as the growth phase. When the growth phase stops, there is a short break before the next cycle, when the hair shaft snaps, the existing hair falls out and a new hair takes its place. As the growth phase for arm hair is programmed to stop growing every couple of months, the hair stays short. Whereas head hair is set to let hair grow for years at a time, so the hair can grow very long (although *Guinness Book of Record* applicants should note there is a natural stopping point between the waist and knee). For most people, split ends only happen on relatively long hair, so your arm hair stays as smooth, silky and split-free as an award-winning shampoo advert – even without the shampoo.

Why do we laugh?

THE KNOWING REPLY
Laughing helps release nervous energy of any kind – and it's good for you!

THE DEEP AND MEANINGFUL
Although we're not strictly the only species that laughs, we are the only ones that make a characteristic ha-ha sound. Gorillas and chimpanzees laugh but more through a system of inhaling and exhaling, while young rats make high-pitched vocalisations when tickled. The laughter of humans, however, is not perfectly understood. Most theories revolve around the idea that laughter is a social glue and helps a group to bond. This is supported by the contagious nature of laughing (see also yawning, p.30). Generally, we laugh when we are happy; when someone else has a defect or breaks conventional social codes, and we get a sense of being better than them; when something is wrong but will not have a disastrous effect on life; and when something is considered wrong or taboo – which all suggest that laughter is the release of nervous or excited energy of any kind. The best news is that laughing is good for you: hooting 100 times is equivalent to 15 minutes on an exercise bike; giggling reduces stress hormones, boosts the immune system and lowers blood pressure; and roaring with mirth exercises the diaphragm and abdominal, respiratory and facial, leg and back muscles.

Why do we cry?

THE KNOWING REPLY
One theory is that it's a way to expel all the physical products - like hormones and proteins - of human emotion.

THE DEEP AND MEANINGFUL
In fact, there are different types of crying. So-called basal tears lubricate the eyes to ensure sharp vision. Tear glands produce 5oz-10oz of basal tears every day which flow over the surface of the eyeball and into the lachrymal ducts in the inside corner of the eyes, and then into the nasal cavity; however, because these tears do not overflow out of the eyeball, they are not usually considered to be crying. We also produce reflex tears, which react to irritants, foreign objects and blows, to help protect the eye's delicate surface. Emotional tears, however, are a different story. No one knows why we turn on the waterworks in response to sadness, anger, humour or frustration, although we are the only mammals that do, excepting gorillas and elephants who have appeared to shed a tear from time to time. The interesting bit is that studies show emotional tears have higher levels of protein and hormones in them, so perhaps they're a way for the body to expel the physical products of emotion. If only your eyes could expel the baggage too!

Why do we dream?

THE KNOWING REPLY

As a way for our brain to exercise. Vs. It's how humans deal with their psychological 'unfinished business' of the day.

THE DEEP AND MEANINGFUL

Medically speaking, dreaming occurs during the REM (rapid eye movement) period of sleep; that is, the period of sleep when our brain activity is at a peak and muscles are temporarily paralysed. The physiological theory holds that dreaming is a way for the brain to exercise during an otherwise dormant period, replacing the brain's daily activity when billions of brain cells are in use. In evolutionary terms, this could have been the brain's way of keeping active and alert to threats, even while asleep. This is supported by the fact that studies measuring the brainwaves during REM sleep are the same as when we are awake, which is not true for other phases of sleep. The other approach is the psychological one, including the theories of Freud and Jung who claim that dreaming is the brain's way of dealing with any unfinished business of the day; or, on a good note, a way of indulging our inner, most personal fantasies in an entirely inappropriate way. Dream on!

Why do men go bald and women don't?

THE KNOWING REPLY
Sorry ladies. You're not nearly as fortunate on this front as you think.

THE DEEP AND MEANINGFUL
Age: there's no getting away from it, and no amount of expensive face cream can cover it up. However, there are bits and pieces of the ageing process that scientists have laid bare, among them baldness. In males, an enzyme called 5-alpha reductase whooshes around the body a few years after puberty and turns much of the accumulated testosterone into a new hormone called dihydrotestosterone. This begins to attach itself to the hormone receptors in male hair follicles, with the uncanny effect that said follicles decide to give up the ghost and wind down production. Initially, this leads to the growth of thinner, weaker hair, but in more than half the world's men over 50, it proceeds to a more terrifying recession than anything the economy has to offer. Baldness can be traced back to its roots as it were, with a strong presence of entire balding families. In women – over 30 million of them in the US today – this presents itself as androgenetic alopecia, triggered by hormone imbalances and stress. What causes balding to pick on the scalp in unknown... scientists are currently tearing out their hair to find the answer.

Why are our eyes different colours?

THE KNOWING REPLY

For in your eye / Lies a natural dye / And so it seems / It's in the genes!

THE DEEP AND MEANINGFUL

You may be surprised to learn that, regardless of the colour of your eyes, it comes from the same source that makes skin tan and hair dark: the pigment, melanin. The kind of melanin that colours the eyes has slightly different molecules which bundle together and settle in the tissue of the iris, and a very thin layer behind that tissue called the iris pigment epithelium. All sorts of things can influence the way our eye colours are perceived by other people, and there are many different grades of each recognised colour. Selective absorption of melanin by haemoglobin and collagen in the blood vessels of the iris, and crystalline formations of melanin in the cells that carry it, can decide the unique hue that we each present to the world. Regarding the genetics: blue is recessive – so a person with blue eyes must have two blue genes in their genetic make-up. If either one of those genes is green or brown, that will make their eyes green or brown. It's possible for someone without blue eyes to have blue-eyed children; but if both parents have blue eyes, their fates are sealed! A blue-eyed life awaits them, guaranteed.

Why do our stomachs rumble?

THE KNOWING REPLY
Ever had air in your plumbing? This is the same thing, only in your guts.

THE DEEP AND MEANINGFUL
Of all The Deep And Meaningfuls in this book, this one goes to depths that others dare not reach! To make this easier to picture, imagine a fairly normal scene that you can readily relate to like, hmmm... being stuck at your desk at work at about 12:55pm, thinking about how lovely that crusty baguette sandwich you're going to purchase in about 10 minutes is going to taste. And then...grrrrooooowwl. A noise like lava gushing out of a fiery gateway to hell emerges from somewhere beneath your belt, and you're stared at accusingly by your colleagues. You have perpetrated this undignified biological faux pas because a trigger in your brain has decided that you are hungry, and this has made the walls of your intestines contract and push everything you've eaten further down into the bowel. This provides room for your baguette sandwich, and the vacated space fills up with assorted digestive gases and fluids, which churn around when the contractions hit. So technically, it's your intestines rumbling. Doesn't really have the same ring does it?

Why do we sneeze with our eyes shut?

THE KNOWING REPLY
The eyelids usually close on reflex. Some strange folk stare through a sneeze, prompting them to find another way to stop spray going in their eyes.

THE DEEP AND MEANINGFUL
Most people believe that if you keep your eyes open when you sneeze, your eyeballs will be propelled across the room at 100mph and lost forever. As it would be a pain to find your eyes if you couldn't see them, it's good to know that this momentary blindness is part of the human system of reflex. While the majority of us remain forever blinded to the truth (bar experimenting with eyelid scaffolding), a small minority of sneezing starers can prove that, in their case, seeing really is believing. Thankfully, for them, the muscles and nerves which attach your peepers to your head are just too strong to break.

Wildlife wonders

FROM WHY ARE THERE NO GREEN MAMMALS?
TO WHY ARE FLAMINGOS PINK?

Why are there still monkeys on the Earth if we evolved from them?

THE KNOWING REPLY
We didn't evolve from monkeys. The theory of evolution goes that we evolved alongside them and are branches of the same tree.

THE DEEP AND MEANINGFUL
Adam, Eve and their good counterparts aside for a minute, the evolution of monkeys, chimps, apes, and our good selves, needs to be viewed like the branches of a tree. The theory goes that our hominid ancestors, together with chimp ancestors, branched from the Great Ape lineage about seven million years ago. Chimps and humans now share about 98.4% of our genetic make-up. The gorilla last shared a common ancestor with us about 10 million years ago and is genetically 2.3% distant from both chimps and us. We branched from orangutans about 15 million years ago, from gibbons about 20mybp (million years before present), and from the old world monkeys about 30mybp. Chimps and humans took millions of years to evolve, during which time many of our ancestors became extinct. In this line of thinking, if we don't destroy the world first, who knows what will have survived millions of years from today…

Why do domestic horses need shoes if wild ones can manage without?

THE KNOWING REPLY
Human requirements have screwed domestic horses' hooves up,
while wild horses still know what's best for their own feet.

THE DEEP AND MEANINGFUL
In the wild, horses managed quite happily without shoes, but when they began to be domesticated their hooves wore down more quickly than they could grow back, and so they were shod. In Asia, horses' feet were wrapped in hide or even plant material. The Romans fitted leather and metal coverings over their horses' hooves, fastened with leather straps. During the Iron Age, horses used in farming needed to be sure-footed and they were shod with iron shoes nailed to their hooves. Well before the end of the first millennium shoeing horses was common throughout Europe. Meanwhile, over on the plains, the wild mustang was happily taking good care of his own hooves. The average mustang has to travel up to 20 miles a day to find water, so his hooves wear down naturally. However, studies show that if unshod horses don't exercise regularly, their hooves will need trimming every 4-8 weeks. Or it's off to the farrier for some new shoes...

Why don't birds fall out of trees when they sleep?

THE KNOWING REPLY
For creatures that can fly in their sleep, locking claws on a branch is nothing.

THE DEEP AND MEANINGFUL
When a bird lands on a branch, tendons in its legs pull the claws into a closed position, thereby locking it onto its perch. When the bird wants to do a runner (or a winger, as the case may be), it 'stands' up, the tendons unlock and it's free to fly away. As a general rule, birds only sleep in the nest when the young ones are at home. The rest of the time they sleep wherever they like. Many birds sleep on branches, far away from most predators. While others sleep standing on the shore, or floating in the water. Some can even sleep while they are flying! This is possible because most birds can let half their brains sleep while the other half is awake – a truly extraordinary feat, also common in whales and dolphins. The scientists call it 'unihemispheric sleep'. We call it sleeping on the job.

Why do cats dig their paws into things before lying down on them?

THE KNOWING REPLY
It's all about kitty-puss being regressive, not aggressive. You might have noticed the same sort of things in some human beings as well.

THE DEEP AND MEANINGFUL
Cats do this in response to their kittenhoods, in which they pawed at their mothers' bellies while suckling, in order to speed up the flow of milk. When cats start scratching the furniture, this is a form of territorial communication or marking behaviour. Scent and sweat glands in between the pads of the paws mix to produce a unique smell. When claws are scraped down on a surface the scent is deposited and the combination of the mark, discarded claw husks and the smell provides a strong visual and scent message to other cats. Call it residual muscle memory, call it force of habit, or call it plain endearing, it seems there are some things a moggy just can't leave behind.

Why do dogs walk around in circles before lying down?

THE KNOWING REPLY
A comfortable bed helps sleeping dogs lie.

THE DEEP AND MEANINGFUL
The common theory is that dogs walk around in circles before lying down in order to mark their territory. In their imaginations, they're creating little, invisible rugs – presumably with little, invisible trespass alarms – that enable them to say: 'This spot's mine.' The extended theory is that you can't take the wolf out of the dog, no matter how much selective breeding goes on. One of the relics of a dog's throwback behaviour stems from the way its wolf ancestor made circles to flatten down the pack's bedding at night. This guaranteed a comfortable night's sleep, and a clear look-out post if any predators arrived. Who'd have thought your poodle had such a wild side!

Why aren't flies blinded by the sun if they have all-round vision?

THE KNOWING REPLY
The crystal-like formation of the fly's eye helps diffuse the light of the sun.

THE DEEP AND MEANINGFUL
Although approximately half a fly's brain is dedicated to visual processing, its vision starts to peter out after about 24 to 36 inches. However, each eye has a special composite cellular structure, which not only allows the fly to stabilise its flight path, evade predators and chase fast-moving airborne targets (and you, of course), but also helps each surface diffuse the light. The lack of any retina type structure, as utilised by humans, means that flies can pretty much fly straight into the sun without blinking so much as an eyelid – if they had any that is.

Why are there no green mammals?

THE KNOWING REPLY

Firstly, mammals have an inability to appear green – most green wildlife you see is a trick of the light. Secondly, being dappled provides better camouflage.

THE DEEP AND MEANINGFUL

Mammals – like humans – can only make two kinds of pigment: black or brown melanin and the reddish-yellow pigment that redheads have. While some frogs, birds, insects and lizards appear green this is just an illusion of the light. Smaller amphibians and insects do well to look green, as they can hide easily on or under a leaf; while colour sensitive birds who mostly fly in a blue sky are thought to have adopted these colours more for mating than disguised flight. Even the many-coloured chameleon is playing tricks with the light and our eyes. Most mammals are far bigger than the singular green items in their landscape like blades of grass and leaves. Plus most mammals and their predators do not have good enough vision to register the importance of the colour green. Which is all good news for the camouflaging spots, stripes and dapples of the tiger, leopard, zebra and gazelle. Excluding the three-toed sloth, the whale and the dolphin, which grow green algae on their backs, the only incidents of bright green mammals occurred in 1995, with the case of the copper-contaminated cat; and more recently in Japan, with three green mice.

Why are flamingos pink?

THE KNOWING REPLY
It's a simply matter of you are what you eat.

THE DEEP AND MEANINGFUL
Most animals are of a certain hue because they are genetically predetermined to be that colour, but flamingos are commonly and crowd-pleasingly pink because of the food they eat. Most of their daily diet is blue-green algae, insect larvae and crustaceans like brine shrimps; these food types contain pigments called carotenoids that turn flamingos red or pink. If they are deprived of a diet high in this pigment the pink colour will fade away, which has tempted some zoos and park owners to supplement their diets with a rose-tinted additive. Humans also eat carotenoids, found in carrots and beetroot for example, but it would be impossible for us to ingest a large enough quantity for us to turn pink. Most mortals have to rely on blushing to get a rosy glow, although some foolish beings have mastered the lobster effect. Not such a good look.

Why do pigeons bob their heads?

THE KNOWING REPLY
It's all in the eyes.

THE DEEP AND MEANINGFUL
Like most prey animals, pigeons have eyes on the sides of their heads. They 'bob' so that each eye sees two nearly simultaneous views and can thereby give an approximation to binocular vision. You can try this yourself by covering one eye and moving your head from side to side. For an animal with side-mounted eyes, forward movements result in 'parallax shifts' – apparent motion of near objects relative to distant ones. Vertebrate eyes, and retinas, work much better with completely stationary images; so while the bird's body walks on, the head is temporarily left behind to stabilise the image and jerked forward at the start of the next step. Owls and humans, by contrast, have front-facing eyes (binocular vision), and thus, no parallax requirements while walking. Heavy-headed creatures with side-mounted eyes – pigs and cows, for example – for whom the avian solution is impractical, have apparently grown to enjoy parallax shifts. And let's face it, it would be pretty impossible to do an impression of a pigeon without all that bobbing around.

Why don't you ever see baby pigeons?

THE KNOWING REPLY
Junk food makes them grow up fast, or you're not looking in the right place.

THE DEEP AND MEANINGFUL
The common street pigeon builds a nest just like your average bird. However, pigeons, living up to the urbanologists' nickname flying rats, are a little sloppier and a little more devious than the average avian. They construct small, flimsy nests, barely large enough to hold Mother Pigeon's usual two eggs, in cornices, on window-sills, under bridges and other out-of-the-way places. While the eggs incubate (for about two weeks) the nest is kept constantly covered, by the male during the day, and by the female at night. Once the little suckers hatch, they spend two weeks in the nest, feeding off a protein substance called pigeon's milk secreted from the crop of either adult. When they're all grown up and flapping, they hit the road – hopefully.

Why do insects have hair?

THE KNOWING REPLY

Hair is considerably more important to an insect than to a human, although not half as attractive in some folk's eyes.

THE DEEP AND MEANINGFUL

Hirsute insects are no laughing matter. They don't grow dodgy goatees, backcomb, dye, braid, crimp, gel or torture their locks purely for fashion's sake. Instead, insects use their hairs for all sorts of genuinely useful, sensory and life-saving functions. For example, flies' furry feet allow them to cling to smooth surfaces and hang on the wall; thousands of tiny hairs help distribute the sticky secretion they use to hold on; pollen sticks to the hair on a honeybee's back legs and is collected into a special area called the pollen basket; and the water beetle's leg hair helps push it through the water. Other insects use their hair as ears, picking up vibrations in the air. In the same way, hair can provide a sense of touch, notifying the insect of the presence of other objects. Bees even use their hair to tell whether they're the right way up - the hairs can sense the direction of gravity and determine what position they are in. And we thought a mohawk was clever!

Why do camels have humps?

THE KNOWING REPLY
It's all just a big lump of fat!

THE DEEP AND MEANINGFUL
Contrary to popular belief, a camel's hump is not a big water sack for the camel but contains mostly fat, as well as some water. This store of fat allows the camel to live without food for up to two weeks, a rather handy option for the desert dwelling camel. Humans and other animals store their fat mixed in with muscle tissue, or in layers beneath the skin – camels are the only ones who keep it all in a hump. When they are away from food supplies for days on end, they can burn fat from their hump to give them energy. Don't feel sorry for the camel though; according to Rudyard Kipling the Camel got its hump because it was too lazy to work. Even though the Ox, the Dog and the Horse tried to get him to help out he just said 'hump-hh' and stood around in the desert even more. Apparently, Man didn't mind but the Wizard was appalled and gave the Camel enough food supply on its back to allow it to work for three days. Work-shirkers, you have been warned.

Why do moths only come out at night if they like the light so much?

THE KNOWING REPLY
It's a sweeping generalisation - not all of them are nocturnal.
Most are just up to a spot of moonlighting.

THE DEEP AND MEANINGFUL
Endless nights on the tiles don't suit all moths - and, in the case of some species, only the male flies at night. It remains to be discovered whether or not Mr and Mrs Moth can change shifts to see a bit more of each other. What can be determined is that moths are phototactic, meaning they're attracted to light, unlike the negatively phototactic cockroaches, which can be chased into cracks with the aid of a household torch. The great majority of moths are nocturnal, and have a love of light for a very good reason - it helps them to find their way around. One theory states that moths calculate their flights according to the earth's rotation, which they gauge by checking the moon. As such, every light that they see at night time looks like the moon, and this may explain their chaotic behaviour when they trap themselves in your bedroom. They are simply confused about why the 'moon' is so close. Okay, it sounds funny - but you imagine thinking every light bulb was the moon...

Cryptic catchphrases

FROM WHY DO WE SAY BLESS YOU?
TO WHY DO WE FEEL BLUE?

Why do people say 'You can't have your cake and eat it too'?

THE KNOWING REPLY
Obviously, this was once a very large cake.

THE DEEP AND MEANINGFUL
The main thing about figures of speech is that they're not meant to be taken literally – and just as well, for this is certainly one of the more risible formulations of the English language, although no one really knows where it came from. First published in *John Heywood's Proverbs* in 1584 as 'Wolde you bothe eate your cake, and haue your cake?', when this mother-hennish phrase is clucked at us our natural inclination is to ask: 'Well, what else am I going to do with it, you jerk?' The idea behind its metaphorical meaning is that one cannot use something up and still have it to hand – which seems fair enough. However, more recently, it has been used by free-wheeling phrasologists as a warning or an 'I told you so' for people who think it's okay to have situations both ways. Another version of the phrase, which focuses more heavily on repercussions, is: 'Eat your cake and have the crumbs in bed with you.' Now, that's uncomfortable.

Why don't words like 'couth' and 'shevelled' exist when their opposites do?

THE KNOWING REPLY
Some of these words did exist, but have disappeared along the away.

THE DEEP AND MEANINGFUL
Language experts call kempt, mantled and couth unpaired words – or negative words that don't appear to have positive opposites. However, there's no blanket answer for why they should be so. Couth was once in general use, stemming from the Old English cunnan for familiar – hence, anyone who doesn't fit in is uncouth. Gruntled was drawn directly from the word grunt, as in the noise of discontent, but the added dis was meant to emphasise the negative rather than form an opposite. Dishevelled is not, strictly speaking, an opposite – it came from the Old French word *deschevelé*, which later became corrupted. Kempt, like couth, actually existed, having come from the Old English kemb for comb – when the root-word fell into disuse around 1600, its opposite was left standing as a synonym for unrefined. Mantle was an Old French verb for donning one's cloak. Optimists will be pleased to note that, in most cases, there is a positive side to everything – even if it's been temporarily lost along the way.

Why is phonetic spelt with a 'ph'?

THE KNOWING REPLY
It's all Greek to us.

THE DEEP AND MEANINGFUL
For the same reason palindrome isn't a palindrome, onamatopoeic isn't onamatopoeic, symmetrical isn't symmetrical, and a fraction is actually a whole word, the history of language is littered with inconsistencies and unexplained occurrences that lend it an endearing charm. One theory goes that when spelling was standardised, words of Greek origin were given an authoritative 'ph' where there was once the Greek letter 'phi'. This included *phonetic*, meaning vocal sounds (from the stem verb to speak); *photo* (from the stem word for light); *philo* (from the stem for for love); and *sopho* (from the stem word for wisdom). Apparently this decision helped certain words retain a certain classical importance. A stem theory in itself, is that the Romans actually heard 'p-hi' when they started writing Greek words even when the Greeks diverted to 'fi' – much to the consternation of some English, German and French folk who must use 'ph' to this day – and to the glee of the Spanish who managed to get away.

Why is abbreviation such a long word?

THE KNOWING REPLY
It stems from the Latin *ad breviare*, meaning to shorten.

THE DEEP AND MEANINGFUL
Always one to sit on their laurels (when they weren't wearing them, that is) and find the short cut, the Romans needed a way to express 'short, low, little or shallow' and so came up with the Classic Latin word *brevis*. Then, they came up with the matching verb *breviare*, which when placed after the word *ad* became 'to shorten'. Through slovenly speech and writing habits, or perhaps a penchant for making new words, this eventually became *abbreviare*. Between 300AD and 700AD the past participle of this produced the Late Latin word *abbreviationem*. Between 1400 and 1600, it gave way to the Middle French version, abbreviation, which, along with the French invaders, found its way into everyday English. So, ironically, a word for making something shorter, just grew and grew and grew...

Why do we say 'I've been working like a dog', when dogs just lie around all day?

THE KNOWING REPLY
We should say: 'I've been working like ye olde dog.'

THE DEEP AND MEANINGFUL
While a lot of domestic dogs treat the world like their own private lounge, history shows they were designed, and very able, to get stuck to the job at hand. Key examples of mutts at work include tracking dogs, load-pulling dogs, military working dogs, bull-controlling dogs and, of course, sheep dogs. The well kept, pampered and lazy pup about town is largely a modern creation... a luxury spawned by affluence and security. However, some dogs are keen to uphold the working ethic; in addition to guide dogs for the blind and deaf, some dogs have even joined the FBI. It's a dog's life, hey...

Why are captains of ships called 'Skipper' when all they do is stand there?

THE KNOWING REPLY
They're not skipping. It comes from the Dutch word for ship.

THE DEEP AND MEANINGFUL
As Holland was, historically, a seafaring nation of great global importance (as anyone who's read *Moby Dick* will know), the Dutch word for barge-master, *aakschipper*, passed into maritime lore and came out the other side as the Anglicised Skipper. The term went on to permeate baseball, becoming the team-manager's title, with 'on deck' as the in-term for the next batter and 'in the hold' for the man after that. In fact, much of naval language has its roots in Flanders: cruise stems from *kruisen*, meaning paths to cross; smuggle comes from *smokkelerr*, deck is from *dek*, meaning covering; *boom* is the Dutch word for tree; buoy harks from *boei*, meaning to shackle; and ahoy comes from *hoi*, or hello. It took us ages to *fadom* all that out!

Why do magicians only make things disappear into 'thin air'?

THE KNOWING REPLY
Shakespeare has a lot to answer for in language, and this is one of them.

THE DEEP AND MEANINGFUL
Things are much harder to retrieve from thick air. It's glutinous, almost like syrup, and in greater concentration can be as treacherous as quicksand. In 1926, the famous magician, Rudolph Schadenfreude the Great, performed a show at the London Palladium in which he made his wife, Madeline, disappear into thick air. Unfortunately, she became trapped, and the combined might of Rudolph and all his friends couldn't free her from the spiritual quagmire. After that, any magician who used thick air as a vanishing aid was plagued by the sound of Madeline's voice calling out for help – a curse that left many magicians psychologically scarred. As a consequence, the Magic Circle outlawed thick air in 1930, and any magician caught using it was liable for heavy fines. Actually the above is all a load of thick air. In fact, just like critical, leapfrog, majestic, dwindle and pedant the words stem from Shakespeare: in *The Tempest* 'thin Ayre' was used to describe the disappearance of something. Now away with you, into thin air...

Why do you call out 'Shotgun!' when you want to ride in the front seat?

THE KNOWING REPLY
To get the best seat, obviously.

THE DEEP AND MEANINGFUL
In fact, the history of calling 'Shotgun!' goes back to the days of covered wagons and the Wild West. On a trip across the plains, the driver of a wagon would hold the reins of his horse team and concentrate on driving. This left him and the occupants of his wagon susceptible to sneak attacks from bandits and thieves. To avoid this atrocious circumstance, it became necessary for one person to sit next to the driver with a shotgun and fend off the enemy. Defending against bandits is no longer the sole priority of 'Shotgun!' however, but it has evolved into a pre-driving ritual that is experienced before almost every car ride across America and even the world. However, some people do take 'Shotgun!' very seriously, so if you haven't got a bullet proof vest you should be aware of the following: there is no crime greater than calling 'Shotgun!' on Monday, in reference to a prearranged lift on Friday; if you call 'Shotgun!' after someone has sat in it, you'll have a fight on your hands; and never, ever, ever overlook 'The Hand Rule'.

Why do we call them 'apartments' when they are all stuck together?

THE KNOWING REPLY
And why do we call them 'flats' when there's space inside them?

THE DEEP AND MEANINGFUL
Even though apartments are in the same building, they're all split up – by those fabulous, solid, brick objects known as walls. So the living spaces are 'apart'. And that's as small, compact and flat an answer as we could find.

Why do we say 'bless you' to people when they sneeze?

THE KNOWING REPLY
To keep all those modern day plagues at bay.

THE DEEP AND MEANINGFUL
The origins of this phrase stem from the days of the plague, when people would say 'God bless you' as a means of stopping people developing the disease if they sneezed – often the first sign of it rearing its ugly head. These days, sneezing doesn't usually warn of something as vile as the plague, but we still say 'bless you' anyway, and the custom persists in many cultures – albeit with different words. The Germans say Gesundheit, meaning 'Good health to you'; the Indians shout 'Live!' which elicits the rather catchy response, 'Live with you!' from the sneezer; some Scandinavian countries use the term 'Prosit!'; while in some Muslim societies sneezers thank Allah with the phrase 'Alhamdulilah'. What is strange is that some groups see sneezes as omens used by the Devil to detract from prayer (along with little birds, apparently), while others, like the Indians, find those who can't sneeze the biggest threat of the day. Good news in Delhi for hayfever sufferers, then!

Why do we say we 'feel blue' when we feel down in the dumps?

THE KNOWING REPLY
So sailors of old could share their sorrow with the rest of the world.

THE DEEP AND MEANINGFUL
If you are sad and describe yourself as 'feeling blue' you are using a phrase coined from a custom among old deepwater sailing ships. If the ship lost her captain or any of the officers during her voyage, she would fly blue flags and paint a blue band along her hull when returning to home port. Feeling 'down in the doldrums' also stems from sulky seafarers. 'The Doldrums' was an area near the Equator where light winds made life tough for sun-baked crews, so for nautical dwellers it was the most depressing point on Earth.

Why do they call it 'head over heels' if our head is always over our heels?

THE KNOWING REPLY
Like many things, it got turned upside down.

THE DEEP AND MEANINGFUL
'Head over heels' - generally means one has fallen madly in love in an impetuous and unconstrained way - is actually a corruption of 'heels over head', which dates back to the 14th century and makes a lot more sense. After all, how can you fall head over heels when we spend most of our waking lives in that position anyway (acrobats need not apply). The corrupted version became inverted around the end of the 18th century, it seems as the result of a series of mistakes by authors who didn't stop to think about the conventional phrase they were writing. The two forms lived alongside each other for most of the next century – the famous Davy Crockett was an early user of the modern form in 1834: 'I soon found myself head over heels in love with this girl'. But as late as the beginning of the 20th century L Frank Baum consistently used the older form in his Oz books: 'But suddenly he came flying from the nearest mountain and tumbled heels over head beside them'.

Why do we say 'the living daylights' as an expression of anger or fear?

THE KNOWING REPLY
Unfortunately, the history of language fails to shed any light on this one.

THE DEEP AND MEANINGFUL
The word 'daylights' was used in the 18th century to mean one's eyes. The first example on record is from 1752, in *Amelia* by Henry Fielding: 'If the lady says such another word to me... I will darken her daylights'. It extended its meaning through the following half century to mean any vital part of the body, not just the eyes. So a sentence like 'they had the daylights beaten out of them' would mean that the persons concerned suffered severe injury. There are many examples in the 19th century of expressions like 'knock the daylights out of him' or 'scare the daylights out of him', and in the later 19th century the term was expanded to 'living daylights'. Since one's daylights are always alive, this does seem to be an unnecessary addition, but then logic has never been an influence on the creators of words and phrases. Perhaps more logical is the phrase 'having the living daylights robbed out of you', which stems from the days when British windows were painted to avoid tax. Daylight robbery indeed.

Why do we say 'It's raining cats and dogs' to describe a torrential downpour?

THE KNOWING REPLY
Although other animals have fallen from the sky,
'cats and dogs' are just a good way of describing how heavy the rain is.

THE DEEP AND MEANINGFUL
Although there have been cases of frogs, toads, fish, alligators and even monkeys falling from the sky, outbursts of descending household pets is based in mythology. In Northern lore, cats are traditionally associated with bad weather and are supposed to have a great influence on it. Sailors also apparently adhere to the cat theory and have a saying 'the cat has a gale of wind in her tail' to describe a particularly frisky cat. Furthermore, dogs are a signal of the wind, as they were attendants of Odin, the storm god from Norse mythology. Thus, cats brought the rain and dogs brought the wind. Other less likely theories include a corrupted version of a rare French word 'catadoupe' or 'waterfall'; and that in 17th century Britain, when drainage systems were basic, if there was a heavy rainfall the gutters would overflow with debris, including dead animals. Slightly better than raining 'pitchforks', 'hammer tongs' or 'chicken coops' at any rate...

Why do we say 'mind your Ps and Qs'?

THE KNOWING REPLY
Pints and quarts; pieds and queues; pleases and thank yous.

THE DEEP AND MEANINGFUL
This phrase, usually dished out to naughty children by scolding parents, probably developed from parents teaching their little darlings the alphabet. Ps and Qs are easy to mix up, as many children will have discovered. The phrase could also originate from printers ensuring their apprentices did not confuse the easily mistaken letters when handling type letters, which are printed back to front. However, there are more far-fetched theories. One suggests that in pubs, drinkers with a tab running were marked up for how many pints (Ps) and quarts (Qs) they drank. When it came to paying the bill, they were gently or otherwise prompted to 'mind their Ps and Qs'. Another theory holds that in the time of Louis XIV, while large wigs were fashionable, dancing instructors would tell their charges to mind their Ps (feet or pieds) and their Qs (wigs or queues) to make sure they didn't lose their head gear while making a formal bow. Or, as the phrase is usually used, it could just be short for 'mind your pleases and thank yous'.

Why do we say 'sleep tight'?

THE KNOWING REPLY
It has something to do with how the bed is sprung.

THE DEEP AND MEANINGFUL
The most popular explanation behind this phrase is based on the way beds were made before metal bed springs and synthetic fibres were developed. Beds were made of a wooden frame with the mattress laid onto a rope 'net'. To make sure the bed didn't sag, the ropes had to be pulled tight around the frame – hence the expression. However, although this is a pleasing explanation, it's probably not true. In 18th-century England, one of the meanings of the word 'tight' was soundly or well, and so the phrase is merely an archaic way of wishing someone a good night's sleep.

Why do we use an '&' – or ampersand – as shorthand for 'and'?

THE KNOWING REPLY
Because the overworked kids of yesteryear were too tired to speak properly.

THE DEEP AND MEANINGFUL
We owe an etymological debt to bored 19th-century schoolchildren for this longer-than-the-word-it's-short-for word. It comes from a tedious-sounding school drill where pupils had to recite all 26 letters of the alphabet plus the '&' sign, pronounced 'and', which was then considered part of the alphabet. Any letter that could also be used as a word in itself – as in 'A', 'I' and '&', was highlighted in the recitation by preceding it with the Latin phrase *per se*, meaning 'by itself'. Thus, the end of this daily ritual would go: 'X, Y, Z and *per se* and'. In their hurry to get to the end of this parrot-fashion slog, the children routinely slurred the final phrase to 'ampersand', and the term crept into common use. The form of the symbol itself – '&' – is thought to come from combining the letters 'e' and 't' which together spell the Latin word for 'and'. Ampersand we're glad we got that one sorted.

Why do we call a weird or dotty person as 'mad as a hatter'?

THE KNOWING REPLY

Although hatters can be mad, it should be 'mad an an adder'. It's a tad more *Jungle Book* than *Alice's Adventures in Wonderland*.

THE DEEP AND MEANINGFUL

When Lewis Carroll wrote *Alice's Adventures in Wonderland* – where the phrase was most famously coined – he probably didn't know that the mercury salts used in the production of felt hats drove hat makers mad by soaking into their nervous systems. It's more likely that Carroll's Hatter was called 'Mad' because he often hung out with the March Hare, and was therefore mad by association. His appearance – as rendered in John Tenniel's illustrations – may have been based on one of Carroll's acquaintances, Theophilus Carter, an Oxford-based upholsterer with a curious (and curiouser) turn of mind. The phrase already existed as a corruption of 'Mad as an adder'. Adders, being prone to the odd thrashing lunge, were regarded as fairly crackers; and in his 1881 book, *Words, Facts and Phrases*, Eliezer Edwards noted that the Anglo-Saxon word for adder was 'atter' – a mere 'H' short of 'Hatter'. One wonders what Alice would have done if she had come across a mad adder instead...

Why do magicians say 'Abracadabra'?

THE KNOWING REPLY

It was once a serious incantation thought to have magical properties.

THE DEEP AND MEANINGFUL

The exact origin of 'Abracadabra' is unknown, but it probably first appeared in late Latin as a magical word inscribed on amulets worn around the neck to ward off trouble. This was written in an inverted triangle with 'abracadabra' along the top and each of the 11 lines minus one letter, until only 'a' was left at the bottom. The idea was that as the letters diminished, so would the disease or evil. Scholars do not agree on the precise etymology of the word. Some believe the source of the word is the Aramaic 'Avrah KaDabra' which means 'I will create as I speak'. Others suggest it comes from the Arabic 'Abra Kadabra', meaning 'let the things be destroyed'. Or perhaps it has to do with the Hebrew words 'ab' ('father'), 'ben' ('son'), and 'ruach hacadosch' ('holy spirit'). It has also been claimed that the word comes from Abraxas, a Gnostic word for God. Whatever its source, the word was once taken seriously as an incantation before being taken up by stage magicians as a nonsense word to impress audiences. Hey presto! And Abracadabra!

Why do we say 'turn the tables'?

THE KNOWING REPLY
Because the game of backgammon allows for sudden changes of fortune.

THE DEEP AND MEANINGFUL
According to the 1898 edition of *Brewer's Dictionary of Phrase and Fable*, collecting antique tables was fashionable among wealthy men in ancient Rome. When these collectors chided their wives about their expensive shopping habits, the women turned them towards these antique tables and reminded their husbands of their own extravagances, quite literally 'turning the tables on them'. Sadly, there is no evidence that this yarn is true. Instead, the expression probably derives, like other phrases such as 'streets ahead' and 'level pegging', from the game of backgammon. In backgammon, the two sides of the board are often called 'tables', which was also an old English name for the game. One rule of this table sport allows a player to double the stakes in certain situations, regain the upper hand very suddenly and literally turn the tables on his opponent. So, if someone tries to give you one theory, just 'turn the tables' on them with another.

Why do we say 'for donkey's years'?

THE KNOWING REPLY
It's the ears, not the years. Unless you can find a mule to prove otherwise.

THE DEEP AND MEANINGFUL
The most common explanation for the origin of this phrase is that donkeys live long and glorious lives; so to equate a period of time with the life of a donkey is to impress upon people the sheer hugeness of the interval for which you haven't cleaned the fridge, tidied the garage or seen one of your best friends. However, the average lifespan of a donkey is nine years in Ethiopia, 11 in Egypt, 14 in both Kenya and Mexico, and a none-too-scintillating 27 years in England. Even the real codgers, those stubborn mules with staying power, only come in between 45 and 50 - not even a pensionable age! In fact, donkeys should be talking about their longest waits in terms of 'human's years' - or humans should be saying things like, 'I've been decorating this bathroom for Galapagos-turtle's years'. The long and tall of this linguistic mutation is not the 'years' of the donkey but the rather large proportions of its 'ears', conveniently used as rhyming slang.

Why do we say you should 'never look a gift horse in the mouth'?

THE KNOWING REPLY
You'd have to be a saint to come up with such an enduring phrase.

THE DEEP AND MEANINGFUL
It's 400AD, and the critical establishment has already sunk its teeth into society, governing public taste with mere viewpoints. You are a humble theologian with a body of Biblical translations, polemics and treatises to your name, and your latest writings have caused a stir. However, as you consider your work a cultural gift, you shrewdly inform your detractors: *Noli (ut vulgare est proverbium) equi dentes inspicere donati.* And without really knowing it you are responsible for a soundbite that echoes for the next, hmmm, one-and-a-half millennia. You are Eusebius Sophronius Hieronymus, aka St Jerome, and the practice you mentioned in your immortal quip ('Never look a gift horse in the mouth') was how a horse's age could be assessed by a spot of amateur dentistry. As a horse gets older, its gums recede; so in a time when the age of a horse was as important as the mileage on an Audi is today, one had to resort to checking the length of its teeth. However, if someone gives you a whole horse, isn't it a bit rude to quibble over its age?

Why do we say 'okay'?

THE KNOWING REPLY
The word has so many potential origins, it's probably just as curious about where it came from as we are.

THE DEEP AND MEANINGFUL
The most likely origin of this top bit of slang is America. In short, it stemmed from a word from the Choctaw Indians, 'okeh'. It was used heavily by 19th century frontiersmen, and even found its way into the speech of Presidents Jackson, Harrison and Wilson. However, there are numerous other supposed sources. Some say it was an 1830s abbreviation for the misspelling 'Orl Korrect' or a corruption of the African exclamation 'waw-kay' from the Bantu and Wolof dialects used by slaves. Others suggest it comes from: the Liberian 'oke'; the Burmese 'hoakeh'; the initials of the venerable Indian chief, Old Keokuk; the initials of President van Buren's 1840 campaigning nickname 'Old Kinderhook', which were used in the name of his electoral base, 'The OK Club'; a corruption of the French *au-quais*, which described the conditions in which French sailors 'at dock' in the American War of Independence would hire prostitutes; and other linguistic quirks from Finnish, Scottish, Anglo-Saxon, Old English, Prussian and Greek. Okay!

Why is gold measured in 'karats'?

THE KNOWING REPLY
A helpful bunch of Arabic beans lent us this word; and we kept it.

THE DEEP AND MEANINGFUL
Gold has several levels of purity: when it's mixed with another metal, it becomes part of a lighter alloy – so, throughout history, its purity has had to be gauged. In ancient Arabia, this was done with bean pods. Each pod was equivalent to four wheat grains, which was the original standard for measuring the weight of gold. Bean pods, known as *quirat* in Arabic, presumably caught on as they were less fiddly than grains, and so *quirat* became karat as the accepted token of measuring. In our time, only 24-karat (or 24-bean pod) gold is certified pure; while white gold is actually an alloy made with nickel, silver or platinum. It's worth mentioning that the word carat has the same origin, but is used for measuring gems. And carrots, being too cumbersome for currency or weight, are best left for eating.

Why is 'hippopotomonstrosesquippedaliophobia' – the word to describe the fear of long words – so long?

THE KNOWING REPLY
Unless you fear long explanations, go straight to The Deep And Meaningful.

THE DEEP AND MEANINGFUL
Hippopotomonstrosesquippedaliophobia is the combination of elements suggesting largeness or length, deliberately forming a word likely to induce the fear it denotes. It is a truly wicked combination of 'hippopotamus', 'monstro' – the Latin for monster, 'sesquippedalio' from the Latin sesquipedalia denoting things one and a half feet long, and, of course, 'phobia' to force each superfluous syllable into a category of fear. It is unlikely that this 15-syllable contrivance is ever used purely for its meaning. The term 'sesquipedalophobia' is recognised in formal writing; while the four-syllable phrase 'fear of long words' is certainly worth considering too.

Puzzling pastimes

FROM WHY ARE BOXING RINGS SQUARE?
TO WHY ARE SOAP OPERAS SO CALLED?

Why are boxing rings square?

THE KNOWING REPLY

Round rings hark back to the circular boxing rings of pugilist design.

THE DEEP AND MEANINGFUL

In the early days of pugilism, fighters locked horns in circular rings drawn on the ground, but it eventually grew apparent that this two-dimensional design was hardly going to contain them. This was solved, at least temporarily, by planting a series of stakes around the circles – but this proved costly and ran the risk of causing falling fighters unnecessary injuries. So, in 1838, the Pugilistic Society decided that the key to reining fighters in was rope, not posts, and they devised a new fighting platform that continues to this day: a minimum of four posts, lots of rope, maximum fighting space and, yes, a square – although the name 'ring', in honour of the original design, stuck.

Why are there dimples on a golf ball?

THE KNOWING REPLY
The dimples reduce drag which makes the ball fly smoother and faster to its destination. Whether it flies in the right direction is up to the golfer.

THE DEEP AND MEANINGFUL
The answer to this question can be found by looking at the aerodynamic drag on a sphere. For a smooth sphere, this is much larger than the average drag experienced by a golf ball. The reduction in drag is implied because the flow on a dimpled ball becomes turbulent at a lower velocity and remains attached longer than on a smooth sphere. As the speed of the dimpled golf ball is increased, the drag doesn't change much, which is a good property in a sport like golf. Although round dimples were accepted as the standard, a variety of other shapes were experimented with as well. Among these were squares, rectangles, and hexagons. The hexagons actually result in a lower drag than the round dimples but for some reason or another have not yet made it into the shops.

Why do basketballs have black lines?

THE KNOWING REPLY
It's a gripping tale.

THE DEEP AND MEANINGFUL
Basketballs are made from various materials, like polyurethane, PVC or leather, and are comprised of segments known as 'strips'. So, the manufacturer will run off an enormous amount of these strips, which will then be sealed together into whole basketballs. The material that seals the strips together is a black rubber cement, and the rubber seals are known as 'channels'. Some channels are wider than others, but in general they provide the basketball player with another means of grip, different to that of the main material. For example, a player might fit his fingertips into the channels to put a spin on the ball with a flick of his wrist, because the rubber is easier to get hold of than the main covering. Black just so happens to be the colour of the standard rubber that is used in the manufacturing process, although there's no accounting for some countries inconsistencies in width.

Why do women throw 'like a girl'?

THE KNOWING REPLY
Far be it for us to make a flippant toss-up between the sexes, but the court is definitely open on this one.

THE DEEP AND MEANINGFUL
A contentious topic if ever there was one. Without sounding sexist, girls usually throw leading with their elbow and don't use their shoulder, almost pushing the ball; whereas boys tend to use shoulder rotation. Why the difference? Up until about the age of 11 or 12, boys and girls register very similar scores in tests of motor skills and athletic ability. However, some studies show that when puberty kicks in, boys outshine girls in almost all motor skills including being able to throw a ball almost twice as far. This has been put down to the higher percentage of muscle a boy develops - a basic physiological difference between the sexes. However, when another study was conducted where girls and boys threw a ball with their non-dominant hand, that is, right-handers with their left and left-handers with their right, girls threw almost the same distance as boys. This would suggest that boys' supposed superiority is a matter of practice and could be learnt by girls. Are you ready to throw it up for debate.

Why does Superman wear his briefs on the outside of his tights?

THE KNOWING REPLY
20th-century sportsmen are the culprits here.

THE DEEP AND MEANINGFUL
In the first third of the 20th century, it was quite common for athletes to wear shorts over their tights in order to keep themselves 'in check'. Superman was created in the 1930s and, being a man of athletic prowess, was decked out in the attire that seemed reasonable at the time. Said attire became almost as recognisable as his logo, which meant that his image attained the status of a brand. As a result, his pants never made it below the surface, and remain topside to this day. Oh, and if you ever feel the need to start a long conversation, simply get an English person and an American together and strike up a debate about how Superman wears his 'pants'. This is more controversial (and entertaining) than you might think.

Why are tennis games scored 'Love-15-30-40' instead of 'Zero-1-2-3'?

THE KNOWING REPLY
Medieval French numerology has a lot to answer for.

THE DEEP AND MEANINGFUL
In the French Medieval era, 60 was considered a number of beauty and completeness. The scoring structure for tennis games - then known as *jeu de paume* or 'the game played with the bare hand' - was therefore 60. It was split into quarters, although a subtle adjustment was made in order to account for the 'advantage' or two consecutive points that would have to be played in the event of a *deuce* - ye olde French for two. Then, it was judged that after 30 points, the most balanced separation would be to level them all to the nearest 10: the next becoming 40, the advantage-point 50, and the winner 60. A player with the correct lead could win a game straight through from 40, but with 40-all, the 50 would have to be played for. If both players clinched it, the *deuce* would be repeated, and the 50 would have to be played for again. After a time, the '50' point became known as simply 'advantage'. As for 'Love' meaning 'zero', it's thought that this was derived from the French *l'oeuf*, or egg - an object with the physical shape of a nought.

Why is it called a '*matin*-ee' performance if it takes place in the afternoon?

THE KNOWING REPLY

The invention of electrical lighting enabled the original morning 'matinee' to be held in the afternoon; and the afternoon performance in the evening.

THE DEEP AND MEANINGFUL

Derived from the French for a morning occurrence, the misnomer of 'matinee' is now widely accepted as meaning an afternoon performance at the theatre or cinema - even in France. The term did, however, originally mean a morning performance, stemming from the French word 'matin' for the morning. In Elizabethan times the main performance of the day - now held in the sociable hours of the evening - was held in the afternoon, as it was hard to stage a play without artificial lighting. Therefore, the earlier performance would take place in the morning. As electrical lighting developed, theatrical performances moved to the more glamourous evening spot, and earlier performances were staged in the afternoon.

Why don't dice always show a 'six', when 'one' should be the heaviest side?

THE KNOWING REPLY

The pips should be down, but casinos have found a way to beat the bias.

THE DEEP AND MEANINGFUL

The way dice are made and thrown, it's unlikely that they will produce a 'six' every time. Probability just doesn't allow for that kind of success rate; but there is a small bias towards the 'one' landing face-down in most dice - the reason being that the 'pips' are scooped out of the six surfaces, leaving them all differently weighted. It won't happen on every throw, or even often enough for you to notice, but the bias will certainly be bubbling under the surface. Professional gamblers take exception to that sort of thing, which is why casino dice are as straight as you like, and Las Vegas dice are the most impartial in the known universe. Casino dice have their pips filled with a material that is the same density as the dice themselves, and the pips on Vegas dice are flush with the surfaces. So, if the customers complain about their results, they've only got their own luck to blame.

Why do people clap their hands to show their appreciation?

THE KNOWING REPLY
It was thought to be a pre-speech way to show excitement to fellow primates.

THE DEEP AND MEANINGFUL
Behavioural scientists believe that clapping originated from man's distant past when speech had not fully developed. This is supported by watching primates in a state of excitement when they will usually clap and hit their bodies. A highly efficient way of making noise using only your own body, clapping is less tiring then shouting and much noisier than clicking your fingers. However, when it became the norm to applaud a performance, is not exactly known. In Roman society, the Emperor Nero is said to have paid Alexandrian youths to applaud him as his singing was so bad. These so called *claqueurs* (from the French 'to clap') became prevalent in France in the 16th century when French poet Jean Daurat bought up the unsold tickets to one of his plays and gave them away in exchange for a promise of applause. By the late 19th and early 20th centuries, there was a move to get rid of clapping as some composers and conductors thought it disrupted their flow of their work. In Germany a hush became the ultimate in audience sophistication.

Why is it called a soap opera when nobody sings – or washes?

THE KNOWING REPLY

Always quick to see a money-grabbing moment, the first serials were sponsored by slippery soap manufactures. Much like the present day, then.

THE DEEP AND MEANINGFUL

The term actually stems back to the first days of radio, when the main broadcasters of the 1920s realised that they could get advertisers to sponsor a show and so increase their profits. Devoted housewives with a penchant for cleaning were the obvious target. In order to persuade more women to manifest a pre-war soap addiction, radio bigwigs created the daytime serial format. And before we knew it the age of consumerism was born – every network had a serial of their own, sponsored by a tempting cleaning agent, oven scourer or spam in a can. The word opera was taken from 'horse opera', a term used to describe Westerns in the 1920s and before long the catchy phrase had found it's way onto TV. But just before you smugly settle into your favourite soap, happy that you now possess the key to all human existence, consider this – the first radio soap opera was actually sponsored by a margarine company. So, theoretically, you're watching margarine musicals.

Why is Donkey Kong called 'Donkey' Kong when, in fact, he's a giant ape?

THE KNOWING REPLY
'Donkey Kong' stands for 'stubborn ape'. Or it could be a spelling mistake...

THE DEEP AND MEANINGFUL
Shigeru Miyamoto, the Japanese creator of Donkey Kong – the Nintendo computer game which single-handedly spawned Mario and a host of other thumb-twiddling addictions – claims that he and his team looked through their Japanese-to-English dictionary for a name that would be a good English translation of the term 'stubborn ape'. The book gave 'donkey' as a word for 'stubborn' and Kong as a word for 'ape' referring to the character King Kong. Nintendo freaks and computer geeks cite this as the whole truth and nothing but the truth from The Master and Creator; but some cynics believe it was always intended to be called Monkey Kong, but someone just couldn't spell. How it got so far without anyone noticing is anyone's guess! All part of a geeky cover up, no doubt.

Why, when we throw things at people and say 'heads up', do they duck down?

THE KNOWING REPLY
It's only natural to duck down when something is falling on your head, no matter how much you've been warned.

THE DEEP AND MEANINGFUL
Very often, when we throw things at people (in play, not anger), we try pretty hard to lob them, giving them that little bit of top spin and a decent, upward curve. As such, it is most likely that a thrown object will approach its intended catcher from above. Hence the term 'heads up', suggesting in very clear terms that you should look to the sky, see the object falling towards you - usually a 'harmless' football - and, by all means, feel free to catch or head it. Unfortunately, this helpful instruction is frequently misinterpreted as a license to panic, so the catcher is likely to crouch down, hands over head, while the object thuds into the small of their back. Perhaps it would be easier to adapt to the 'heads up' if it wasn't called a football...

Why are playing cards divided into Hearts, Spades, Diamonds and Clubs?

THE KNOWING REPLY
The suits may be of equal value, but their designs are all about class.

THE DEEP AND MEANINGFUL
The fun of card games is drawn from having to pursue cards of certain suits in order to make up stronger 'hands'. The search for these cards, which may be lurking in other players' hands or in the deck, is what gives such games their addictive pace. However, the reasons behind the look of the suits are a bit more complicated. Hearts, Clubs, Diamonds and Spades arose sometime around 1480 and were a hit as they were easy to mass-produce with stencils. The roots of the suits lie in the most prevalent distinctions of the time – those between the upper-crust and 'people who do things'. Stemming from a mixture of Spanish and French archetypes, Hearts stood for the Spanish *gens de chaeur*, or 'men of heart' who were members of the ecclesiastical community; Spades were drawn from the symbol for the nobility, the sword, which in Spanish, is *espada*; Diamonds didn't symbolise gems at all, but tiles, thereby representing merchants; and Clubs came from the French *trèfle*, or trefoil, the mark of the peasantry. A suite of suits, as it were.

Food for thought

FROM WHY DO WE EAT SQUARE MEALS?
TO WHY DO MOST DOUGHNUTS HAVE HOLES?

Why does the last piece of ice always stick to the bottom of the glass?

THE KNOWING REPLY
Melting water on the ice cube and water or liquid on the bottom of the glass are drawn to each other so they 'stick' together – and the ice cube with them.

THE DEEP AND MEANINGFUL
Outside the freezer, the surface of an ice cube is in a constant state of flux. Ice cubes have an ability to sublimate, or evaporate from a solid directly into a gas, skipping over the liquid stage completely. An ice cube that has been swimming around in your drink will be in an even more excitable state, coated in a residual sheen of moisture from the tipple you've just quaffed. This coating will cling to the ice cube thanks to a trick known as water surface tension. The molecules on the surface of a liquid are always attracted to those at the centre, allowing the liquid to 'seal' itself; but if you edge two drops of water towards each other, their attractive forces will make them combine into one. In a drinks glass, the sheen on the ice may be considered as one unit of liquid, and the moisture at the bottom of the glass another. The surface attraction between these units of moisture draws them together into one – so the last ice cube 'sticks' to the bottom of the glass.

Why do we eat a 'square meal' from a round plate?

THE KNOWING REPLY
The expression 'square' was used in America to denote reliability, satisfaction and value for money, and so was any meal of that ilk.

THE DEEP AND MEANINGFUL
The phrase 'square meal' does not seek to describe any angularity in the actual food - although you might want to watch yourself with the crispy edges on your roast potatoes. Decent, honest, straightforward, proper, sturdy, bona fide: all these descriptions come under the umbrella of the now largely defunct expression 'square'. The newer figurative meaning is quite different - and most unflattering - but the American original equated with reliability (in people), satisfaction (in product), and value for money (in purchase). This was eventually applied to any plate-load of filling nosh, its first known print reference appearing in the *San Francisco Trade Herald* in August 1878: '...to get the sugar [money] for a good square meal'.

Why isn't chocolate a vegetable when it comes from a cocoa 'bean'?

THE KNOWING REPLY
Chocolate is to the cocoa bean, what sugar is to cane.

THE DEEP AND MEANINGFUL
Cruel as it may seem to dash the hopes of chocoholics by barring their favourite food from the realm of more nourishing things, it just has to be done. Chocolate is no more a vegetable for coming from beans than sugar is a plant for coming from cane. Orange juice is not fruit, it is merely the juice of a fruit. Milk is not cow, but the, er, the juice of a cow. All these foodstuffs are derivatives of original, natural resources, and no amount of wishing that chocolate was a vegetable in order to feel better about munching great chunks of it will make it so. And that includes trying to pass a Chocolate Orange off as a fruit.

Why is an ice-cream sold with a flake called a '99', not a 'number 1'?

THE KNOWING REPLY
It's a homage to the number of elite guards enlisted for the Italian Monarchy!

THE DEEP AND MEANINGFUL
In 1928, a Cadbury executive called Mr Berry came to County Durham and grew curious about the activities of the local Italian ice-cream makers. These gelato aficionados were trying to increase sales of their products by offering novel incentives, like sandwich wafers with slabs of ice-cream nestled between them. Berry saw an instant market for a Cadbury product that would fit in these ice-cream sandwiches, and set about finding the best one. The Flake, already produced in a large size, seemed like the obvious choice and was soon issued a smaller, cheaper version specifically for the sandwiches. The Italian ice-cream makers loved it, and over time the sandwiches were replaced by cornets full of soft ice cream with Flakes planted in them like flagpoles. Their 99 name was derived from the Continental connection: in the Italian Monarchy, the ruler had an elite guard of 99 men - so, in honour of the ice-cream makers' heritage, the new Flake was named a 99. In terms of taste, though, it comes first every time.

Why do we call them banana trees when bananas grow on bushes?

THE KNOWING REPLY
We keep slipping up on this one: it's because they look like trees.

THE DEEP AND MEANINGFUL
In fact, they're herbs cunningly disguised as trees. Humans can be very simple, and when they see something that looks like a tree, they think it's a tree. However, you only have to run your hand over the banana plant's trunk to discover that it's not made of wood and bark, but comprised of a tightly wound core of leaves. This makes it ineligible for the tree family, and puts it among the shrubs. Whenever bananas are cut down, new stalks and shoots appear a few months later from the root systems left in the ground. To our immense good fortune, these root systems form new banana plants for up to 100 years, making bananas one of the planet's most sustainable resources. This answer also provides a fine opportunity for a change in perception: because the plant is a herb, bananas themselves are berries. Now let's not have any more banana slip-ups after this, okay?

Why is it called a hamburger when the burger has no ham in it?

THE KNOWING REPLY
Ich bin ein hamburger. The clue is in the name.

THE DEEP AND MEANINGFUL
Well, it's only Americans who call them hamburgers. Those of a British persuasion tend to call them beefburgers, thinking that the ham is referring to pig. The name is actually said to have come from the German city of Hamburg, where the idea of sticking a piece of meat between two pieces of bread supposedly originated. However, where the idea came from has Hamburger historians in a quandary. Similar snacks have cropped up in Roman texts, although the modern definition of a hamburger (ground meat formed in a patty and placed in a bun) was first mentioned in an American cookbook in 1891. Several American towns claim to be the inventors of the hamburger, including Seymour in Wisconsin and Hamburg in New York. There is also a theory that Tatars developed something similar to a hamburger when they placed beef under their saddles to tenderise it and form it into a patty. Proud German Hamburgers, however, advise all false proclamators to leave well alone, or they might get a knuckle sarnie instead.

Why does milk curdle in the sun but not in a hot cup of tea or a saucepan?

THE KNOWING REPLY
Fresh milk may be alive (with microbes, that is), but it can't think for itself.

THE DEEP AND MEANINGFUL
Fat globules in milk are coated with heat-resistant membranes, and when milk is heated, the surrounding proteins stick to those membranes and make them even stronger. If this were not so, many culinary delights that we take for granted, like thick *béchamel* sauce, would be impossible to make. When you add milk to your tea or coffee, these fat globules fend off the heat and keep it smooth. If milk is left in the sun, however, the sunlight causes a reaction between riboflavin vitamins and the amino acid methionine, which contains sulphur. The reaction doesn't just unleash the sour smell of 'offness', it also affects the proteins, preventing them from acting as they normally do under heat. That's why sun-drenched milk splits off into clumps of fat and protein known as curds and dregs of thin liquid called whey. If you want to see fresh milk curdle in your tea or coffee, add a few drops of lemon juice. The citric acid will spoil the milk's chemistry and its proteins will clump together. Delicious.

Why is vanilla ice-cream white when vanilla extract is brown?

THE KNOWING REPLY
Even though vanilla pods are brown, they don't have enough colouring in them to turn the ice-cream the same hue.

THE DEEP AND MEANINGFUL
The vanilla bean, the only edible fruit of the orchid family, a reputed aphrodisiac and the world's most intensive and expensive agricultural crop, has been prized since the days of the Aztecs, and used as a flavouring for everything from chocolate to cigars and, of course, ice-cream. Although vanilla pods don't have enough pigment in them to actually turn the ice-cream vanilla coloured, black or brown specks in the mixture usually indicate that the real thing has been used – a rare occurrence these days, as according to one source, 97% of vanilla used as a flavour or fragrance is synthetic. Anyway, how else would you know which one was chocolate?

Why is it called an eggplant when there's no egg in it?

THE KNOWING REPLY
The first discovered eggplants were small and white and looked like... eggs!

THE DEEP AND MEANINGFUL
Like the tomato, the eggplant or aubergine is a fruit (actually a giant berry) that is eaten as a vegetable. Although we think of it as the quintessential Mediterranean food, it came to Europe via India, or, some say China. The earliest eggplants were round and white, shaped like, you guessed it, eggs – hence the name. And, in fact, these small white eggplants are starting to appear on our shelves again. Which answers that burning question: Which came first, the aubergine or the egg?

Why is it called a pineapple when there is neither pine nor apple in it?

THE KNOWING REPLY
What else do you call something that looks like an overgrown pine cone and tastes like an apple?

THE DEEP AND MEANINGFUL
In 1493, Columbus and his crew were introduced to the *anana* by the fierce Carib peoples who had spread its cultivation up the islands of the West Indies. The Carib had learned of this plant and taken its name from the Guarani, tribes living in the Amazon basin. When the Spanish got their hands on this tasty morsel, they called it *piña*, basically because it looked like a large pine cone. And the English added the word apple due to the similarity between the flavours of the two fruit. It would seem that either the pineapple or the apple must have tasted much different back in those days! Although another theory goes that the word apple was in fact a generic term in Ye Olde English used to describe all fruit. Which begs the question, if apples were the only fruit, what then were oranges...

Why do doughnuts have holes?

THE KNOWING REPLY
Not all of them do, but the hole-less ones can fall prey to soggy centres.

THE DEEP AND MEANINGFUL
In the 16th century, doughnuts, which originated from Dutch bakes, didn't have holes. Instead they were deep fried battered cakes, which had soft, almost soggy centres. These travesties were called *olykoeks* and the hole was an American modification that, once introduced, redefined the shape of the pastry. Aside from making them easy to hold on your finger, the hole removed the soft, soggy centre and produced the doughnut that is loved by millions of people all over the world today. Which genius came up with the delicious jam filling is another question altogether.

Why is a sausage in a bun a hot dog?

THE KNOWING REPLY
Well, what's so frank about a furter?

THE DEEP AND MEANINGFUL
Somewhere in the late 19th century, students from Yale started to refer to wagons selling sausages in buns as 'dog wagons' (yes, the concept of hot dogs have been around that long). Apparently, they were a little suspicious about the contents of the sausages, a fear that still lives in the hearts of anyone who has resorted to the economy sausage. Once the students were referring to them as dogs, it was a short step to hot dog, a term used in the *Yale Record* in late 1895. Another theory suggests that when sausages in buns were first becoming popular, a cartoonist in New York immortalised them as dogs in buns because he couldn't spell the word frankfurter. However, the cartoon didn't appear until 1906 so the theory was blown away as quickly as you could say fast food. Some also say that hot dogs were called frankfurters, until World War One when anti-German sentiment led to the name being dropped like a hot potato in favour of the more Anglophone hot dog. More to the point, can you really eat one without ketchup or mustard; is it really worth it without onions; and does a hot dog taste better if you get it from the street or if you make it yourself? It's a hot dog debate.

Why do we eat popcorn at the cinema?

THE KNOWING REPLY

Snack entrepreneur Sam Rubin brought popcorn to the cinema in the 1930s and it's been 'pop-ular' ever since.

THE DEEP AND MEANINGFUL

The blame for cinemas charging outrageous prices for boxes filled with air, fake butter and burst maize, for sticky carpets underfoot and tender celluloid moments ruined by other people's chomping jaws can be charged to one Samuel Rubin. Back in the days of early cinema in the USA, the flickers appealed largely to the working classes. Trudging home after a 10-hour workday, they would stop off at a nickelodeon for a few minutes' cheap entertainment. Some smart entrepreneur realised that these audiences had worked long hours with only a 30-minute meal break and began to sell popcorn to hungry viewers for a nickel a bag. Samuel Rubin was just 12 years old when he went to Oklahoma in 1930 and saw popcorn being sold in a cinema. On return to New York, he started selling popcorn in movie theatres. Owners resisted having popcorn machines in the theatre because of the smell and mess, so 'Sam the Popcorn Man' bagged the popcorn and delivered it to cinemas. Later, owners realising that the smell of popping corn was enticing to customers. Soon, warm popcorn was selling faster than hot cakes.

Why does alcohol make us drunk?

THE KNOWING REPLY
Blame it on the ethanol, a chemical that causes us to act in very strange ways.

THE DEEP AND MEANINGFUL
The active element in alcoholic drinks like beer and wine is ethanol, a chemical compound easily absorbed into the bloodstream that reaches the brain very quickly. Initially it causes the release of endorphins, or feel good chemicals, and stimulates the cortex, hippocampus and nucleus accumbens – areas of the brain which control thinking and pleasure seeking. There is also an increase in metabolism in the areas of the brain associated with movement, which explains all that over exuberance. However, ethanol has a depressant effect on the areas of the brain that control planning and motor learning, meaning areas of the brain responsible for thinking and pleasure seeking start to slow down. Ethanol also induces the gamma-aminobutyric acid system (GABA), which inhibits activity in the brain and is thought to be responsible for impaired memory; it inhibits the metabolism of glucose in the brain, which is what causes blurred vision; and it affects the organs responsible for balance. Chances are you don't need a book to tell you all this as you're probably testing the effects of ethanol as we speak.

Why does mint taste cool?

THE KNOWING REPLY

Menthol tastes cool for the same reason that ice feels cold.

THE DEEP AND MEANINGFUL

Starting with a bit of basic science, different chemicals have different effects on the human brain, and all the food we eat contains a staggering amount of them – even the stuff with no additives or preservatives (they're just the E-numbered icing on an already overstuffed cake). In mint, what you might call the active ingredient is the popular, multi-purpose chemical called menthol. This chest-soothing, nose-unblocking compound has a molecular structure that registers with a series of sensitive strands in nerve cells known as ion channels – or, more specifically, the channels codenamed TRP-M8. Whenever you hold an ice cube in your hand, its temperature sets off the TRP-M8 channels, which send messages into your brain that enable it to think of the cube as cold. What menthol and ice have in common is that they both have an effect on the same part of the nervous system. That's why if you drink mint tea or smoke menthol cigarettes, the cool effect still comes through. That doesn't mean it's cool to do.

Why do curry and chillis taste hot?

THE KNOWING REPLY
It's a sprinkling of molecules, a stirring of nerve cells and a dash of electricity.

THE DEEP AND MEANINGFUL
When we accidentally touch a hot oven and say words to the effect 'Goodness me – that smarts', we have just had something on our nerve cells tickled: something called an ion channel. The channel that's activated by hot temperatures is called TRP-V1, and it sends signals to the brain that allow it to register a particular object as hot. However, it's not just heat that does this: the reaction can also be stimulated by chemicals. In chillis, the chemical that tantalises the TRP-V1 channel (which you won't find on cable) is Capsaicin, which gives us Capsicum, the generic name for all kinds of peppers. In certain studies, some kinds of pain have been shown to have an effect on the heat-sensing TRP channels, which may explain why some people find spiced food completely intolerable. It may also explain why we develop a light-headed, giddy sensation whenever we eat such food. To calm its stimulated nerve channels, the body releases its very own painkillers, endorphins, which charge through our bloodstreams hell-bent on calming things down. Since this is an entirely natural process, a chilli-high can only ever be good news.

Why is it called a 'Full English Breakfast' when there's no 'Full English Tea' or 'Full English Dinner'?

THE KNOWING REPLY
To distinguish it from *le competition*.

THE DEEP AND MEANINGFUL
In the late 19th century, once the industrial revolution had swelled middle-class coffers, foodstuffs from the hot evening meal started to appear at breakfast. This was a means of expressing contentment and not a little gluttony for those who were able to afford it. Then, in the 1960s – under the influence of all things chic – the breakfast went minimal, or rather, Continental, shrinking down to a mere bread roll and a humble cup of tea, coffee or juice. The Full English became a marketing buzz-phrase to get people interested in the greasy world of egg, sausage and bacon again after the Continental had threatened English society with culinary annihilation. The phrase never included tea, or dinner, which were already full enough – and never stood a chance at midday due to the increasingly popular Light Lunch.

Tall traditions

FROM WHY IS THREE THE MAGIC NUMBER?
TO WHY DOES THE EASTER BUNNY CARRY EGGS?

Why is three the magic number?

THE KNOWING REPLY
Choose a personality. Pick an answer.

THE DEEP AND MEANINGFUL
Although De La Soul had a winning attempt at rapping their way to the answer, the discourse on this one is so vast each theory has been attributed to a personality instead. In this case you should: soothe a mathematician's head by reminding them that three is a prime number, divisible only by itself and one; show a physician a simple triangle or point out that the earth is the third planet from the sun; de-frazzle a biologist who believes everything comes in twos with the news that we only really need the heart, the brain and the body to live; comfort mothers-to-be with the Blind Melon lyrics, 'A man and a woman had a little baby... And there were three in the family'; satisfy neo-classical scriptwriters and spindoctors with place, action and time – Aristotle's three unities; confiscate the paintbox from artists who don't know their primary colours; and for the theologians, there is always the Holy Trinity and that optimistic trio, faith, hope and charity. It also pays to note, however, that like those unfortunate blind mice, bad luck and buses also come in threes...

Why do buses come in threes?

THE KNOWING REPLY

Crowded bus stops mean even evenly-paced bus schedules will get messed up.

THE DEEP AND MEANINGFUL

You know the drill; you've been waiting at the bus stop for what feels like about an hour, when all of a sudden three buses trundle up together. Studies have shown that it does really happen. Although buses stagger the times they leave the depot, circumstances along the way can have a dramatic effect on their schedules. If there are lots of passengers at stop No. 1, bus No. 1 will be delayed while they all get on board, allowing the bus behind (bus No. 2) to catch up. And since bus No. 1 has already picked up all the passengers at stop No. 1, bus No. 2 won't have to stop and so will catch it up quicker. Once bus No. 1 has picked up all the passengers at stop No. 1, it is running a bit late and so more passengers will have congregated at stop No. 2, meaning bus No. 1 is slowed down even more to allow on passengers at stop No. 2, allowing bus No. 2 to catch up again. This only needs to happen twice for a threesome of buses to gather. The only place it doesn't happen is in Cuernavaca in Mexico where buses are unregulated and go when they want. Phew!

Why do superheroes wear Spandex?

THE KNOWING REPLY
Where would a superhero be without a good dose of stretching the truth?

THE DEEP AND MEANINGFUL
Spandex is easy to clean with a warm, damp sponge and a dry tea towel. It can be folded for concealment in a briefcase or sports-bag – depending on the luggage preference of the superheroes' alternative identity. It can be worn beneath a business suit or casual clothes with no obvious, giveaway signs – unless the alternate identity has left the house with an open collar or unzipped fly. It can be sewn in such a way as to allow for convenient bathroom activities – the idea that superpowered saviours would deprive themselves of the ability to go to the toilet is an urban myth that should be purged from hero lore. Spandex is also very flexible – which comes in handy when its wearer is locked in a wrestling match with the marauding Monster of Titan, or undergoing the exertions of propping up a falling bridge. It can be printed with logos or go-faster stripes and, being skin tight, is very difficult for enemies to grab hold of while showing off all those superhuman muscles (assuming that this is the source of the superhuman strength). Maybe the real question is: Why do professional cyclists all dress like superheroes?

Why is Friday the 13th unlucky?

THE KNOWING REPLY
There's been a lot of bad luck on Fridays and 13ths.

THE DEEP AND MEANINGFUL
Ancient Scandinavians were the first to give Friday a bad name. Having ascribed the fish emblem to their love or fertility goddess, Freyja, they offered the aquatic creatures to her in abundance on Fridays and indulged in frantic bouts of ritualistic hanky-panky. Unfortunately, said hanky-panky got rather out of hand and, before long, Friday was no longer a day they looked forward to – goodness knows what they go up to. Meanwhile, 13 was comprehensively stitched up by the Last Supper, as this was the number of people present at that fateful Christian buffet. Then the day and number became allies in early 14th-century France, following a feud between the French King, Philip le Bel, or The Beautiful, and Pope Boniface VIII. The spat began in 1305 after le Bel tried to cure French fiscal woes by taxing the church, and ended with the Pope's death after a spell of house arrest. The Beautiful then tried to join the luxury-laden Knights Templar, but they rejected him, and he ordered their arrest on Friday 13 October 1307 – and that's how this black day for the Knights became black for us all.

Why are black cats considered lucky?

THE KNOWING REPLY

In fact, most of the world is split over the fortune brought by a black cat.

THE DEEP AND MEANINGFUL

It is only in certain parts of the world that black cats are lucky. In Britain and Japan, a black cat crossing your path is a sign of good fortune, but in the USA the opposite is the case. In China there are those who believe black cats to be harbingers of famine and poverty. While Latvian farmers, who find black moggies in their grain silos, dance with joy, believing they will bring a good harvest. Superstitions around cats have existed for thousands of years, perhaps because they have lived so closely with humans for so long. The Egyptians worshiped them (killing a cat was a crime punishable by death), and the Romans also considered them sacred. It was in the 17th century that black cats became associated with witchcraft – witches were thought to have 'familiars' and what more likely creature to channel supernatural powers than a cat, the colour of darkness and magic itself? Or as Arundhati Roy's novel, *The God of Small Things* suggested, they could all be 'black-cat-shaped holes in the universe'. How lucky you when you see one depends on what you find on the other side...

Why does the Easter Bunny carry eggs?

THE KNOWING REPLY
Easter features many Christian and pagan symbols,
and if you roll them up together you get a chocolate-carrying rabbit.

THE DEEP AND MEANINGFUL
Our reasons for celebrating Easter falls into several camps. For some it's the most important date in the Christian calendar when Jesus died and was resurrected; for others it's a chance to holiday without using any annual leave; but for most it's an excuse to indulge our senses in an unadulterated choc-fest, preferably the egg-shaped, bunny-delivered kind. The thing is, we all know that bunny's don't lay eggs, so how did this happen? In this instance it seems to be the egg that came first, adopted by the ancient Greeks and Romans as a symbols of fertility. In 2nd-century Europe the predominant spring festival was a raucous celebration of the Saxon fertility goddess Eostre, who was symbolised by the hare. Some believe the hare became the bunny and hey presto, it's eggs of fertility all round! The legend of the egg-laden Easter bunny is further compounded by the 17th century German tradition of Oschter Haws. Adopted by German settlers in the US state of Pennsylvania, this customary rabbit is now believed to be responsible for coloured eggs in nests worldwide. Or it could just be the chicken's day off.

Why are there 'Twelve Days of Christmas' when there is clearly only one?

THE KNOWING REPLY

Some say it's a catchy Catholic catechism, some that it was a memory and forfeits game; while the partridge-loving French believe it came from France.

THE DEEP AND MEANINGFUL

Various camps of belief surround the 'The Twelve Days of Christmas'. One explanation is that it was designed as a catechism by canny English Catholics to keep their faith and themselves alive during the protestant clampdown between 1558 and 1829. Under this line of thinking, the 12 gifts in the song represent various Catholic teachings, such as the 'partridge in the pear tree' being Jesus on the Cross. However, this story falls apart as the spiritual significance of the song applies to Protestants too. Meanwhile, over in France, there exists three versions of the song, which point to it originating there; plus the 'partridge' was not introduced to England until the late 1770s. The first English version appeared in 1780, listed as a memory-and-forfeits game in a children's book *Mirth Without Mischief*. The object was to sing along without mixing up any of the gifts; a mistake that could cost a kiss or a candy. Cunning Casanovas are considering extending the Days of Christmas to 100…

Why does breaking a mirror mean seven years bad luck?

THE KNOWING REPLY

A combination of Greek prediction, Roman health cycles and Italian snobbery has laced many a dressing table disaster with woe.

THE DEEP AND MEANINGFUL

Back in the 6th century BC, the Greeks began using a shallow bowl filled with water to predict the future of the person who cast his image on the reflective surface. If one of these 'mirrors' broke, the seer would automatically predict that the person holding it would die. Later, in the 1st century AD, the Romans adapted this superstition and added their own twist to it. Since they believed that a person's health changed in cycles of seven years, a broken mirror indicated seven years of poor health and misfortune. That belief was reinforced in 15th-century Italy, where the modern mirror was first manufactured. Since mirrors were expensive at the time, those who were wealthy enough to afford one told their servants that breaking the fragile treasure would result in seven years bad luck. Which means that worrying about seven years bad luck for several times as long, has all been in vain.

Why is there a song about London Bridge falling down when it still stands?

THE KNOWING REPLY
Blame the Vikings.

THE DEEP AND MEANINGFUL
In 1009, a Norwegian Viking, Olaf the Stout, found his progress up the Thames barred by London Bridge. So Olaf had great mats of willow and pliable wood made, and placed them over his ships so that they reached down over the gunwales. Under these he had timbers set up as thick and high as possible, so that there was room for the swinging of swords and the screen was strong enough to withstand stones. When the fleet was ready, they rowed up the Thames to London Bridge. While lesser ships were damaged under the barrage of stones and had to withdraw, Olaf's ships rowed right up under the bridge and tied ropes around the piles that supported it. Then they rowed off downstream with all their might, shaking the piles until they loosened. When the piles broke away, the bridge burst asunder and consequently many men fell into the river. Might have known the Vikings had something to do with it.

Why do UK general elections always seem to be held on Thursdays?

THE KNOWING REPLY
Despite the majority of Europe opting for Sunday, Thursday was the day when working Brits were thought to be sober enough to vote.

THE DEEP AND MEANINGFUL
General elections are traditionally held on a Thursday in the UK, but there is no law that dictates they must be held then. Across Europe elections are held on Sundays; France, Germany, and Spain opt for Sunday voting to maximise turnout. However, in the UK, every election since 1931 has been held on a Thursday. Before then there were a variety of election days including Saturday in 1918, Wednesday in 1922, and Tuesday in 1932. The first election on a Thursday was in 1918. The exact reason why politicians stuck with Thursdays has been lost in the mists of time, but the story goes that Thursday was the day of the week when working men were most likely to be sober and therefore able to navigate their way towards a ballot box. Weekly pay was handed out on a Friday, so Friday nights were dedicated to drinking. Thursdays were therefore the peak time for sobriety, as most men were coming to the end of their weekly cash and couldn't afford to drink.

Why use Champagne to christen ships?

THE KNOWING REPLY

Champagne replaced wine, which replaced early human sacrifices of blood.

THE DEEP AND MEANINGFUL

Ships were originally christened to bring them and their crew good luck and to appease the gods before entering the dangerous seas. The practice goes back to Viking times when the christening was not with Champagne but with human blood. The christening involved the spilling of blood and human sacrifices – all part of a normal offering. In Ancient Rome and Greece, sailors splashed water to purify the ship. But it was during the Middle Ages that wine began to replace blood and was splashed on the boat as it entered the water. By Tudor times an elaborate ritual had sprung up around the christening. An important person sat on deck and was presented with a precious goblet filled with red wine. After sipping the wine, said dignitary was expected to say the ship's name and spill a bit of wine on the deck. The goblet would then be thrown overboard. Goblets were abandoned in favour of bottles in 1690, and once Champagne was well known and held in high esteem, it replaced wine. The blood was a bit messy and didn't taste great anyway.

Why is touching wood lucky?

THE KNOWING REPLY

It's from ancient rituals and beliefs, where wood had special powers.

THE DEEP AND MEANINGFUL

There are several theories surrounding this phrase. Some people think it goes back to pre-Christian rituals and practices where certain types of wood - especially oak, ash, hazel, willow and hawthorn - had special protective powers; therefore to touch wood was a special charm. Some people believe that the sound of touching or knocking on wood stops the Devil from hearing whatever rash and defiant statement you have made: 'I've never been hit by a car before. Touch wood.' The Devil will therefore not hear your arrogant claim and you will continue to cross the road safely. This could stem from Christian beliefs that touching wood is akin to touching the cross, thereby protecting you along the way - as long as you have a handy wooden crucifix in your pocket. Touching MDF, laminate, or your friend's head, doesn't apply.

Why do we salute magpies?

THE KNOWING REPLY
For good or bad, black or white, there are plenty of reasons to salute.

THE DEEP AND MEANINGFUL
Firstly, it's not all bad for magpies: in some circles, a single magpie sitting on a roof means that the building will never fall down – which is great if you can't bear to rope in the builders; ancient Chinese wisdom tells that that the magpie saved the Manchu people (forefathers of the Qing Dynasty) and is a symbol of good luck that should never be killed by humans; while the Koreans take it as a bringer of inspiration. However, in the UK there are some notable counterpoints: a single magpie circling a house is said to be a portent of death; and a lone one seen in any circumstances is supposedly a harbinger of bad luck. To ward off their negative influence, some people salute them with a tip of the hat and the phrase: 'Hello, Mr Magpie – where are your wife and children today?'. Others follow this ritual by spitting over their left shoulder three times. At least the rhyme 'One for sorrow, two for joy, three for a girl, four for a boy', gives the magpie a fair try.

Why do we shorten Christmas to Xmas?

THE KNOWING REPLY
It's just an ancient Greek abbreviation.

THE DEEP AND MEANINGFUL
First it's necessary to clear up the potentially offensive misreadings of this shortening. The letter X does not stand for Christ because it looks like a wonky cross, nor is the word Xmas an attempt to secularise the festival even further by removing Christ from its very title. In fact, the use of this shorthand is nearly as old as Christianity itself. The first letter in the Greek word for Christ is 'chi', which looks like the letter X in the modern Roman alphabet. Hence Xmas is indeed a perfectly legitimate, if somewhat lazy, abbreviation for the full word Christmas. In the same line, 'Xian' is also sometimes used as an abbreviation of the word Christian, although where is not clear! As an added bonus, the Greek alphabet is also the reason why the fish is used as a symbol of Christianity. The first letters of the declaration *Iesous Christos Theou Yios Soter'* (Jesus Christ, God's Son, Saviour) form the acronym 'icthys', which is Greek for fish.

Why do we have pumpkins and bobbing for apples at Halloween?

THE KNOWING REPLY
Celtic traditions carved the way for today's fun and games.

THE DEEP AND MEANINGFUL
Halloween, as we know it today, stems from a combination of the ancient Pagan festival Samhain and a ritual observed to oust evil spirits before a Roman Catholic invention, All Hallows or All Saints Day on 1 November. The apple bobbing comes from Celtic traditions and was originally conceived for unmarried people at social gatherings. Apples, which are a symbol of fertility and love, were placed in a tub of water and potential lovers would try and catch one in their mouths. The first successful 'bobber' would be the next person to get married. Carving pumpkins goes back to an ancient Irish tradition. Jack was a lazy farmer who tricked the Devil into promising to never let Jack into Hell. The Devil agreed, but when Jack died he was too sinful for Heaven. However, as Hell was out as well, he wandered the earth looking for a resting place, carrying his lantern made from a carved turnip. He was known as Jack-O-Lantern and when pumpkins were introduced to Europe from the Americas, they replaced turnips as lantern material of choice.

Why is Santa's suit red?

THE KNOWING REPLY

Illustrators decked out St Nicholas in a variety of hues, before settling on red.

THE DEEP AND MEANINGFUL

This is best answered by probing the origins of the Man in Red. Saint Nicholas, the herald of the secular Father Christmas, came from Dutch folklore and was adopted as Patron Saint by the New York Historical Society in 1804, in honour of the city's Dutch past. In European folklore, Nicholas had been moved aside by an image of the infant Christ, Christkindlein, who gave gifts to children with a dwarf helper, Belznickle. These two characters were eventually merged into one, Kriss Kringle, who gradually blended with the American Saint Nicholas. Drawings of Nicholas and Kringle had shown the figures in a huge variety of shapes, sizes and garbs. In 1881, Thomas Nast's Merry Old Santa Claus cartoon made Santa into a kindly old man; and in 1885 he was decked out in red on a set of American Christmas cards. This image was co-opted by Coca-Cola for a 1930s ad campaign and, thanks to brand-power, the cloak stuck. So while Christmas has traditionally evoked a biblical and pagan combination of red, gold and green, Santa himself has been something of a karma chameleon. Maybe that's where Boy George got his inspiration for the song...

Why do we tie tin cans to wedding cars?

THE KNOWING REPLY

In fact, we should be throwing our shoes after the bride and groom.

THE DEEP AND MEANINGFUL

In the main, shoes have been thought to bring good luck all over the world and there are a number of superstitions relating to them. This may be a throwback from the Middle Ages when footwear was expensive and the common practice was to bequeath it to members of the family. The saying 'Following in your father's footsteps' is thought to have arisen from this custom. In this case, tying shoes to the back of the honeymoon getaway car has become a tradition normally considered the work of a prankster. In Anglo Saxon times, the bride was symbolically struck with a shoe by her groom to establish his authority. Brides would then throw shoes at their bridesmaids to see who would marry next. Then, in Tudor times, guests would throw shoes at the newlyweds' carriage. To ensure good luck, the shoes were later tied to the carriages, which due to cost or consumption have been replaced with tins and cans today. The Victorians then came up with the rhyme: 'Something old, something new, something borrowed, something blue...'. This ends with: '...and a sixpence in your shoe', to help bring wealth to the newly married couple. Probably where some folk go wrong.

Man-made mysteries

FROM WHY ARE THERE 60 SECONDS IN A MINUTE?
TO WHY ARE MANHOLES ROUND?

Why doesn't the glue stick to the inside of the bottle?

THE KNOWING REPLY

Most glues are designed to dry out or react with the air when squeezed out in order to stick; when protected by the bottle, it can't actually 'glue'.

THE DEEP AND MEANINGFUL

Certain glues dry out in order to hold things together, which is another way of saying that they contain solvents that evaporate as soon as they are squeezed out. This evaporation leaves concentrated layers of hardened chemicals behind. Others actually draw upon elements of the air and react with them in order to produce adhesive compounds. By shielding glues from interactions with the air, bottles keep them fluid and ready for use. Not such a sticky question after all.

Why do men and women button their clothing on different sides?

THE KNOWING REPLY
Ladies-in-waiting, side-saddlers and swash-bucklers all come into play.

THE DEEP AND MEANINGFUL
There are many theories as to how the buttoning habits of men and women diverged. The first and most obvious is that women in high society created the first divide by having dress-maids who buttoned their clothes while facing them. The second is that women riding side-saddle didn't want air gushing through their blouses every time the steed sped up. While on the male side, Cavaliers would unbutton their shirts with their left hands while brandishing swords with their right – like a sort of sword-fighting strip-show. If only men could keep on the right side of women in the same way.

Why is the alphabet in the order it is?

THE KNOWING REPLY
There are theories from A-Z but nobody is entirely sure.

THE DEEP AND MEANINGFUL
The original alphabet was believed to have been developed by a Semitic people living in or near Egypt about 3,000 years ago. This was quickly adopted by their neighbours and relatives including the Canaanites, the Hebrews, and the Phoenicians. The Phoenicians spread their alphabet to other people of the Near East and Asia Minor, as well as to the Arabs, the Greeks, and the Etruscans – and even as far west as present day Spain. The Romans – not ones to miss out on a piece of the pie – took the alphabet from the Greek system in 600BC, including the name which stems from the first two Greek letters alpha and beta. They added some vowels, fiddled around with letters and sounds, and spread it around Europe in pretty much the form we use today (albeit the English adding a 'w' in the 1400s). What's not clear is, why the order? We know it can't be phonetic, as sounds like T and D, or S and Z, are too far apart. Some historians say the Phoenician's first 22 letter line-up has spiritual significance; while others say it developed out of laziness to avoid learning hundreds of pictograms. Which kind of offers the relief that order can come chaos after all. How else would you have *The Alphabet Song*?

Why are there 60 seconds in a minute?

THE KNOWING REPLY
Go way back in time, swim down the Tigris, and meet the Sumerians.

THE DEEP AND MEANINGFUL
The measurement of time was originally developed by the world's first civilisation, the Sumerians, who lived around the confluence of the Tigris and Euphrates rivers. To give you an idea of how mind-blowingly ancient they were, they first dreamt up the way we mark time over 4,000 years ago. They based this upon their so-called Hexigesimal numbering system, drawn from the number 60, which - as you will see elsewhere in this book - is also the number that gave us '15-30-40' for tennis scoring. Some theorists believe that the Sumerians bestowed 60 with mystical attributes that linked it to the Zodiac and other constellations. This laid the foundations for astrology and later, astronomy, albeit through what historians term as 'associative-correlative, non-linear thinking'. On that non-line of thought, while 60 seconds became a minute, and 60 minutes became an hour, it seems not much else has changed over time.

Why is it called a television 'set' when there's only one?

THE KNOWING REPLY
Because the TV is made out of three components that form a 'set'.

THE DEEP AND MEANINGFUL
While this expression is, like many quirks of the English language, difficult to account for, it seems reasonable to suggest that a television set is not, in fact, a piece of equipment, but a collection, enclosed in an eye-catching cabinet that fits in with the aesthetic fads of its day. First, there is the receiver, which picks up and translates live and pre-recorded television signals. Then the translation, in the form of a series of electrons, passes into a cathode ray tube, at the end of which a scanner 'fires' the image onto the inside face of a screen. So, the three major items of equipment are the receiver, the tube and the screen. Not one piece of gear, but a kit; in other words, a set.

Why do some countries drive on the left while others drive on the right?

THE KNOWING REPLY
Even driving is a product of conquer and divide.

THE DEEP AND MEANINGFUL
Some countries just have to be right; ironically, in this case, the one's that don't adopted the custom during their time as a British colony. While cars had not always been invented at the time of invasion, swords had; and in this case walking on the left in Britain meant that protecting oneself and others for the majority of right-handed swordfighters was an easier option. It also meant the scabbard, worn on the left, would have less chance of hitting people. Meanwhile, the French Revolution of 1789 prompted the traditionally left-walking aristocrats to hit the right side of the road (where the peasants were allowed to promenade) in the name of self preservation. Later the left-handed Napoleon spread right rule to the low countries. Countries like Egypt, which was a British colony, resisted the left-rule as they has been conquested by Napoleon earlier; North America changed to right rule as a way of breaking from its initial conquerors. The swinging 1960s nearly even switched the Brits, until they realised that you can be right and left all at the same time.

Why don't boats sink?

THE KNOWING REPLY

Because they're lighter than the volume of water they displace.

THE DEEP AND MEANINGFUL

Its all down to Archimedes - he of the overflowing bath, eureka, and naked street running. What Archimedes realised, one day back sometime in 300BC was the basic principles behind buoyancy. Essentially, if an object is placed in water, it displaces water. The object in the water is pushing down, while the water being displaced is pushing back up on the object. These two sets of forces determine whether or not something will sink or float. Too much up and it will float, too much down and it will sink. When boat builders are working, they ensure that a boat is designed so that when it is immersed in fluid it has a large surface area. This helps disperse the downward force and makes it more likely that the corresponding upwards force is able to result in buoyancy. So, as long as the boat's downward force is less than the upwards force of the water, or as long as the boat weighs less than the volume of water it's displacing, it will float. Contrary to popular belief, a mass of water is actually pretty heavy stuff, and so boats made of dense materials such as metal are still able to float. Just don't try and float a tanker in your bath.

Why are manhole covers round?

THE KNOWING REPLY
To stop them falling into themselves. Vs. It's just easy to make them round.

THE DEEP AND MEANINGFUL
You wouldn't want to drop the cover down the hole, now would you? Well that's the leading wisdom anyway. Apparently, to stop the covers falling down, they are round; as opposed to square or rectangular ones, which have the possibility of slotting in diagonally, meaning you would lose the cover forever. However, what about rouleaux triangles which would also find it impossible to fall into themselves. Or the presence of so many square or rectangle covers. Are these just outdated models, in danger of the ever-present 'man hole cover drop' syndrome? Or is there another reason lurking behind round covers? Other theories hold that circles give a better seal than corners; round things are easier to manufacture; round covers can be rolled along the street; and round covers don't need to be aligned. Either way, we challenge you not to look at at least five manhole covers today.

Why does the camera 'add 10lbs'?

THE KNOWING REPLY
When a 3D object is transferred into a two-dimensional medium, the image will be elongated and so things – and people – appear fatter.

THE DEEP AND MEANINGFUL
When we look directly at an object with two eyes we receive a lot of data to our brain and are able to perceive the image in its true three-dimensional shape. However when an image is viewed either on television or in a photograph, we only see the object as a two-dimensional image. To transfer the image of a person from real life via a camera to a two-dimensional representation, the image has to be slightly distorted. Think of it as the extra dimension being condensed into the image and added as a bit round the edges. Subject to an ever vainer nation one study showed that women appear about 5% heavier than they really are in two-dimensional images. However, if you're worried your camera is lying to you, it may be wise to chomp on a painting instead – after all, it's not surprising these state of the art gadgets are so fattening with all those extras added on.

Why are they called '10 gallon hats'?

THE KNOWING REPLY

It's a Spanish language mix-up about decorative braids.

THE DEEP AND MEANINGFUL

Don't attempt to test this one with a hat and 80 pints of water, because you would be wrong and everyone around you would end up rather wet. The name is often thought to imply the huge size of this cowboy hat – in keeping with portion size, person size and many other things Texan. However, this is an error due to a linguistic misunderstanding by the gringos. The hat is not Texan at all but originally comes from Mexico. When Spaniards occupied the country, they wore sombreros whose wide brims protected their faces from the overpowering sun. Their love of decoration led them to embellish the plain brim with braid and this fad really caught on. Some dedicated followers of fashion wore a hat with 10 different braids. Reasonably enough, this was called a '10 galon hat', 'sombrero galon' meaning 'braided hat'. When the Americans saw the sense of this Spanish headgear and adopted it for themselves, they took its Spanish name as well. Continuing to call it a 10 galon hat, the Spanish 'galon' was soon misunderstood, misspelled and mistaken for the liquid measure. And for that, JR should eat his hat.

Why do cars have speedometers to 160mph when 70mph is the limit?

THE KNOWING REPLY
'In case of an emergency' seems less likely than a marketing ploy to tempt power-crazy drivers to buy the latest souped-up car. And it works.

THE DEEP AND MEANINGFUL
No one knows the answer to this one, but there are many theories including that emergency vehicles may need to go faster than the speed limit and so cars should be made to accommodate this need. There are also some places where there is no speed limit, such as on private property and part of the autobahn in Germany. However, less technical theories attribute more to the human quest for power, using tempting speedometers that go up to 160mph as a canny marketing trick to keep speed-hungry people buying. There is also a theory that innovation should not be capped to restrict car manufacturers. Although this one was probably developed by the very same car manufacturers who help keep those power-crazy nutters on the road.

Why is it easier to swat a fly with a swatter than your hand?

THE KNOWING REPLY
Hands are slower than swatters, and cause greater changes in air pressure.

THE DEEP AND MEANINGFUL
For the very, very deep and meaningful refer to 'Why do insects have hairs' (see P.64). If you can't be fussed, it's probably worth investing in a fly swatter to keep the swarm from interrupting your rest. Basically, flies are sensitive creatures and can feel changes in air pressure, such as those created by a person's solid, sweaty palm swiping with murderous intent towards them. Fly swatters, on the other hand (excuse the pun) are veritable stealth bombs of insect destruction. Their in-built venting allows them to get closer to the fly before being detected. By the time the fly's pressure-sense or eyes have finally cottoned on to the danger, it's too late. The venting also means that a swatter can move more quickly through the air than the average hand, making it much easier to hit a moving, and tiny, target. Unfortunately, shouting 'buzz off' as a way of venting your annoyance, just doesn't work.

Why are the keys on a typing keyboard arranged in the Qwerty order?

THE KNOWING REPLY
It was designed to prevent the first manual typewriters from jamming.

THE DEEP AND MEANINGFUL
The first typewriter, manufactured in 1874, used typebars, or arms with characters on the end. When a character is pressed on the keyboard, the arm swings against an inked tape, which then prints the letter. There are generally two characters per typebar; one that will print if the key is pressed on its own and one that will print if the key is pressed while shift is held down. Typewriters jam when two or more typebars strike at the same time and this was a problem for speedy typists who would press the keyboard, and activate they typebar, faster than the typebar could print. The solution was to develop the so-called Qwerty keyboard, which was designed so that letters commonly found together in words were placed far apart so that the typebars had a chance to fall back before the next one came up. With the ubiquity of computers today, there's no need to use the Qwerty keyboard but it remains popular. Proof that even in the office, it's survival of the fittest.

Why do the numbers on the phone go one way, while the numbers on the calculator go the other way?

THE KNOWING REPLY
Can we phone a friend?

THE DEEP AND MEANINGFUL
No one knows for sure why this configuration came about but there are a couple of theories. When touch tone phones were being developed in the 1950s to take over from the old rotary ones, calculators and adding machines already featured 7, 8, and 9 along the top row. Office workers using calculators or adding machines were extremely nimble at this layout, which was good for speedy data entry but not so great for the new phones which couldn't operate at such high speeds. So phone manufacturers devised a plan to slow down the over enthusiastic workforce by reversing the numbers on the keypad. However, having the number one at the top left of the phone was just easiest to use. Also, when letters were assigned to each key, it made sense to start the alphabet on the top row, as Westerners read left to right and top to bottom. Most calculators stayed the same, although some changed into computers along the way.

And the final question? Why? indeed